He is SPEAKING!

...*Are We LISTENING?*

One woman's journey of
...learning to listen...

God is *SPEAKING!*

Do we take the time to *LISTEN?*

Dear Norma and Christi,

Thank you so much for your wonderful hospitality. My thoughts and prayers will be with you.

Robin Gove

Robin Gove

7-13-15

ISBN 978-0-6151-3789-6

Printed in the United States of America

DEDICATION

I lovingly dedicate this book to my husband

Dave

I had been dreaming of writing this book for many years.
I could not get started until he spoke these words to me,
"Get busy and write that book.
Do not worry about anything else, just write."
This Journey of *learning to listen* has been very long and hard.
I would have never survived without his love and support.
He has given up so much to make my dreams come true.
Thank you, Dave, from the bottom of my heart.

Special thanks to our four sons:

David Jeremiah

Jeremy James

Andrew John

Aaron Joel

Each and every one of them has helped me along this Journey.
They have always been there to encourage me at just the right time.
Thanks, Guys!

Special thanks to Andy and Jeremy who helped with the actual process of getting this book published.
Jeremy introduced me to a friend of his who became my editor.
Andrew took care of all the details of getting this book published.

I AM FOREVER GRATEFUL TO ALL OF YOU!
I LOVE YOU!

ACKNOWLEDGMENT

I am so grateful to **Julie Steingerwaldt**
who took time from her busy schedule to edit this book.
Even though I never met her in person,
I will cherish our times together chatting by e-mail.
Her talent has allowed my dream to come true.
Thanks, Julie

I would like to thank **Laurie Mosher**
and my sisters, **Lois Hatfield, Jack Moore** and **Candy Vogel**
for using their talents to edit the final changes that I made.

Finally, I would like to express my deepest thanks to my son,
Andrew Gove who did everything that was needed to
FINISH

He's SPEAKING! Are we LISTENING?

Thanks, Andrew

Table of Contents

God's Plan

Tiny as a mustard seed was how we began,
and even then God had a special plan,
that we might grow and one day come to Him,
because of His love and His son's death for our sin.

He's watched us grow each day of our life.
He's there in good times. He's there in strife.
His loving arms surround us as each day rushes by.
Some have no time for Him, I ask myself **WHY.**

Peace, joy and contentment are what God will give us,
if we open our hearts and in Him we trust.
In our world that is filled with many trials and sorrow,
He gives us hope for our every tomorrow.

God, our heavenly Father teaches us everyday,
the only way to grow in Him is to read His word and pray.
Sometimes as a father, He must chasten His loving children,
only for our best, that we might be more like Him.

If we have trusted in Jesus, someday in heaven we will be,
Oh what joy will fill my heart, when my Jesus I see,
but while here on earth, God has given us a task,
to tell others of His love and a peace that will last.

Dear Reader,

This is the story of my journey learning to listen to God's voice. Spanning a call to be a missionary, to a call to write, this twenty-year journey was challenging, tumultuous, and deeply frustrating, but also rewarding, awe-inspiring and I would not trade it for anything. God is faithful and does not give up on us. I have come to trust this because many times on my journey I felt like giving up myself. I berated myself for going against what I believed God wanted me to do, but He stuck with me and through many lessons, taught me the true value of listening.

This book was born out of the time I spend daily in conversation with God. I ask Him questions about what I am dealing with in my life and as I read the Bible, verses jump out at me as answers from God. When I was a missionary, it was in one of these sessions that a title flashed across my mind: *HE IS SPEAKING! ARE WE LISTENING?* What does this mean? I wondered.

Yes, it is true that God speaks to us through that quiet, small voice within us and also through His written word, but do we take time and listen? Do I listen? More importantly, do I obey?

Throughout my life one of my greatest concerns was finding my time with the Lord. As a woman I realized that if I would make God a priority in my life, I could handle anything. When I did not, when I relied on my own strength and ignored the voice of God, I would eventually wither and become exhausted.

As a missionary I realized first-hand what happens when we neglect God. We change. We begin to look at the negative in others. You would think that missionaries would have it together and know how to stop and make time for God, but my experience has been that many did not. Many missionaries are on the field for a short time and then they quit for various reasons. I suspect that many were so busy doing the ministry that they did not find the time to have their one-on-one time with God.

Then working in a church I realized that people in any ministry could have the same problem as missionaries. They are so busy doing "ministry" that their time with God can slowly disappear. Their ministry suffers because they are doing it all on their own.

Writing for me has been a way to ensure my daily time with God and also a way to encourage others to make room for this valuable practice every day. Without this quiet time with God, it becomes hard to hear Him speak and even harder for us to listen.

In this book I share my ups and downs of learning this priceless lesson and some of the many other lessons God has taught me along the way. If you have ever experienced a lack of peace in your heart, when you are headed in a direction that is not to God's liking, you know how important it is to listen to His voice. My hope is that this book inspires you to spend time listening to God, because the more you listen, the easier you will recognize His voice and the easier it will be to follow His guidance. Peace is the gift that comes to us when we listen to God and follow the path He sets before us.

God wants to SPEAK to us; we only need to take the time to LISTEN.

Robin Gove

Chapter 1

WHO ME, GOD?

I can do all things through Him who gives me strength.
Philippians 4:13

Who me, God? A simple housewife? Could you ever use me?

In the fall of 1983, these thoughts danced through my mind as I woke up each morning. My heart searched desperately for answers, but deep within me, a soft yet firm voice kept saying, "Be still, and wait patiently for me to work." If God were calling me to do something, I would have to be patient for the moment it would be revealed to me. I realized "waiting patiently" would be hard, but I had no choice.

The days passed at a snail's pace as I waited. For what, I did not know, but inwardly the yearning continued. I could never tell anyone what I was feeling. All I could do was wait and pray.

One fall evening as the golden glow of the setting sun began to fade, my husband Dave and I walked hand-in-hand through the "nature area" of our five-acre property. (We named it that because we let everything grow wild on this two-acre parcel except for a mowed path down the center.) My mind was distant as thoughts and feelings flashed this way and that. Dave's warm, gentle touch on my shoulder startled me. He whispered, "Shh…listen!" The sound of scrambling animals confirmed they had already heard us coming. The crunch of autumn leaves under our feet had warned them of our arrival. Turning slowly, I allowed my eyes to meet Dave's and quietly questioned, "Could we ever leave all this?"

His reply came quickly. "It would be hard!"

How could I ever think of leaving such a beautiful place? My world was perfect right where I was. Dave was well-established in a job that he loved, not to mention the handsome income he provided for our family. God had blessed us bountifully with a wonderful family and a beautiful new two-story colonial home on five acres in the country. Our lifelong dream had already become a reality.

Reflecting on our blessings, we slowly edged our way back to our house and back to reality. As we made our final steps to the front door, Dave exclaimed, "Look!" I turned around just in time to see a deer run across our front yard, so sleek and quick. I marveled at the beauty of this sight and enjoyed the cozy feeling it gave me. As I reached to turn the doorknob, a wave of sentimental feelings flooded my heart. My first thought was to quickly go inside and snuggle into my favorite squishy beanbag chair to revel in our blessed life.

As I sat there, I thought about how we would sit around our fireplace roasting hot dogs and playing games together as a family. The crackle of the logs burning would give me a warm feeling. The smell reminded me of being out in the woods around a campfire. I reflected on the times spent together around our large sturdy pine table, watching the breathtaking view of the glowing sunset.

I could never forget the nights I would gaze out of the bedroom window, waiting with anticipation for the moon to rise. The beauty of God's creation was everywhere. Even seeing the beauty of a snowflake falling gently to the ground in the cold of winter was a wonder to behold. Would anyone want to leave all this behind, as I sensed God was asking me to do?

The days and weeks passed swiftly. All the while I wondered if God was preparing us for a change? I could not explain why I felt this way, but the thoughts persisted.

I AM WILLING!

One morning as the sun's rays beamed around the room, I quietly opened the pages of my Bible. The words touched my heart. Deep within, I began to feel that missions in a foreign land could be part of God's plan for us. If this was true God would need to work in all of our hearts to prepare us!" I asked myself, "Would I be willing to go?"

If mission work was, in fact, part of God's plan, what would happen? Could I leave my family and friends? Could I leave my extended family? Our family was always very close. I wondered if I could leave my sister Candy. We were best friends, always there for each other. Living with a father who was an alcoholic had drawn us closer together. Together we faced the tough times. As we grew up we were married within a year of each other. Our babies grew up together. Many times we bundled them up and walked them in their buggies together.

What about the rest of my family? I had two other sisters, Sharon and Jack, that I truly love. They lived farther away so I did not get to know them as well, but we always had a special bond. What about my Mom? We were so much alike—our personalities and taste in clothing, colors and just about everything else was the same. It would be so hard to say good-bye to her.

The Bible talks about being willing to leave your family and friends. Could I do that? I prayed, "God, you would have to work in a mighty way to give me the strength and desire to do this."

Almost a year had passed when I began to realize that God was not only working in me, but in Dave as well. My heart was being stirred, and God was moving Dave in the same direction. We never shared our thoughts about what was happening within us, because we both felt unqualified to even consider global missions for our family. We were just ordinary people. We had always respected and revered missionaries, never believing we could be missionaries ourselves, so we did nothing about the prompting in our hearts to consider global missions for our family.

GOD BEGAN TO PUSH

God is full of faith. Sometimes the stubbornness of our hearts makes Him give us a little push to get us going in the direction He wants us to go. We may feel unworthy of any task God might ask us to do, but God continues to push in ways that we do not even realize.

In the early spring, we heard about a missionary named Bruce Fleming who would be coming to our church. The bulletin announced that they needed people to host this missionary for dinner. When people would come to our church and needed housing, we enjoyed opening up our home for them to stay, so we signed up for this missionary to come to our home Sunday after church.

As I listened to his stories in the church service, my heart was warmed, and the desire to serve God began to surface again, but the thoughts of being just an ordinary person squelched those desires. While I hurried home after church to finish preparing for our dinner guest, Dave and the kids waited at church to bring this missionary home.

A few minutes later I heard the crackle of rocks under the tires of our car as it pulled into the driveway. As I made my way to the front door to welcome our guest, he had already started to come in the door.

"It is you!" our missionary guest exclaimed when he saw me. I had no idea what he meant. "Whenever I speak in a church," he said, "I always find someone in the audience that I can look to for encouragement, someone who seems really interested in what I am saying. Today that person was you." Suddenly, I knew he could see the desire in my heart for missions.

After a delicious chicken dinner, we talked and listened to this missionary share stories about his life. After ending one story, he added, "There are so many needs in mission today."

"What do you mean?" Dave inquired.

"We need teachers, preachers, dorm parents and construction workers."

"Wait a minute," Dave replied, "Construction workers?"

This comment was a jolt to Dave's heart, as well as mine. He had worked in construction for a few years and did a superb job building an attached garage onto our first house. Without us realizing it, God was using this man in our call to missions.

Hours passed as we soaked up information from our special guest, but then we noticed the color in his face began to fade. His eyelids drooped with fatigue. His forehead became dotted with sweat beads; then he abruptly ran to the bathroom where he began vomiting. Our special messenger from God became very ill. For the next three days he was in our home, sick. In fact, he was so sick that he could not eat. He stayed in bed the whole time. I teased him that it must have been my cooking, but God used this time in a special way in our lives.

As I brought soup and crackers to his bedside, I looked at this frail weak man differently. He was just an ordinary person, like me! He was not a super human-being. He got sick and he needed help. Those three days passed, and God spoke to our hearts in a very special way. If God wanted to use us, He would give us what we needed to get the job done, even if we felt unqualified.

COULD GOD USE US?

In the weeks to come, Dave and I finally began to share our thoughts with each other. Dave asked me, "Do you think that God could use us on a mission field somewhere? Would you be willing to go?"

I shared how I had been burdened about missions for a long time. "Yes, I would be willing," I replied. We sat side by side; our hands clasped together and began to pray. "Dear God, we are willing to go wherever you want us to, just open the door and lead us."

In the moments that followed, joy and fear simultaneously flooded my heart. I inwardly asked, "Could you really use me, Lord, a simple housewife from Stoughton, Wisconsin?"

We spent weeks praying and then inquired about short-term

missions through our church denominations missions' organization. It was the same mission organization our special missionary friend was with. Within days, the information we requested arrived. Feeling strongly that we should pursue this direction in our lives, we trusted God to close the door if this was not His will.

As we looked through all of the information about short-term mission assignments, we considered the different countries that had needs. Our hearts were pulled in two different directions: Africa and the Philippines. We decided to leave that decision in God's hands as we began the first step in our missionary journey.

The application to become short-term missionaries was our first big challenge. Pages upon pages of information needed to be compiled. We had to take a personality test as well as a marriage compatibility test. Since we felt so sure we were to do this, we were motivated to finish the task in a timely manner. When the application was finally completed, we prayerfully sent it in.

It seemed like an eternity before we heard anything and then, several weeks later, the phone rang. I could hardly contain my excitement as the mission's director asked if we could come in for an interview. Before he could say another word, I quickly responded with a resounding "YES!" The date was set. The next step in our missions journey had arrived.

Life is filled with many little tests that continually fall into our laps; soon, we were given our first test.

In preparation for our trip up to Minneapolis, Minnesota for our interview, we packed the car and sent the kids to Grandma's. Everything was set. When Dave arrived home from work, he greeted me with a puzzled look on his face.

"What is the matter?" I asked. He hesitated and then replied, "You will never believe what happened today. I was offered a job that would be the career advancement that I have been looking for. My dream of being in management could finally be a reality. Guess what, the offer is in the city we are heading to this very day, Minneapolis!"

The drive seemed endless. We talked and talked the whole way. "God, what is happening?" we questioned. Confusion overwhelmed our hearts. When we finally arrived at our hotel we knelt together and prayed as we had never prayed before in our lives.

"Dear God, we want your will, not ours, in our lives. We know this job offer could just be a test, to see where our hearts really are, but we do not know, Lord. It is in your hands. Please show us."

When time came for our interview, fear and excitement were battling for control of our hearts. The small office looked like any other office, except for the large world map hanging neatly on the wall. Two empty high-back chairs stood at attention in front of a beautifully polished solid oak desk. When we walked into the room, a man stood up briskly and reached out his hand to welcome us.

Sitting down, we began sharing our life with this stranger. Soon, the warmth of this man made us feel at ease. After we talked for a while he said, "The two countries we have in mind for you are either Africa, working in construction, or the Philippines, working in church planting." Church planting involves starting up new churches in different areas. These were the two choices we felt led to as well.

The interview went well and we were accepted as short-term missionaries. The next step was to make a decision between Africa and the Philippines. On the way home, we knew without a doubt that God was leading us into missions. When God makes His path clear and you make a decision in the direction you believe God is leading, peace overflows in your heart. We had complete peace that this was God's plan for us.

Turning down the job offer would not be hard for Dave since we knew we were following God's leading in our life. We would now have to trust Him to lead us to the country where He wanted us to go.

PRAYER IS THE ANSWER

Again, prayer was the much-needed ingredient in our lives. Dave and I prayed and asked God to show us without a doubt where He wanted us to go." Africa was where Dave's abilities in construction could be used. We did not feel qualified to work in church planting in the Philippines, so we were leaning toward Africa. However, we needed God's guidance in our decision.

I will never forget the bright, sunny day when God answered our prayer in a definite way. I was sitting on our bed having my quiet time with the Lord. Dave was downstairs in his massive tan chair doing the same thing. As I was studying God's Word, a specific verse spoke to my heart.

"He has saved us and called us to a holy calling, not according to our works, but according to His purpose." —2 Timothy 1:9

As I read this verse, my thoughts focused on the words "not according to our works, but according to His purpose." Perhaps going to Africa would be according to *our* works, not according to God's purpose. Could God be using this verse to lead us to the Philippines? While I prayed about this verse, Dave walked into the room.

With a smile on his face that warmed my heart, he looked at me and his face was beaming. As he pointed to his Bible he said, "Look at this verse, 2 Timothy 1:9." After reading the entire verse to me, he continued, "Do you think God could be using this verse to help us make the decision to go to the Philippines? We could make a decision according to my work, but that might not be God's purpose."

My voice cracked as I said, "You will never believe this, but God has shown me that very same verse and given me the very same thoughts."

Our decision was made; God had truly answered our prayers. The next step in our missionary journey would be the hardest task of our life, but we knew we would not be traveling that road alone. God would be there with us.

Chapter 2

THE LONGEST YEAR

Be still before the Lord and wait patiently for Him.

Psalm 37:7a

Our journey to becoming missionaries was at times a dark and fearful road with many curves and bends. Many times we wondered if we would ever reach our destination, but we knew who the driver was and we could do nothing, but trust that He would get us there on time.

The first stop on our journey was candidate school: two weeks of intensive study on missions and preparations for our two-year stay in the Philippines. At times we felt so small to be allowed to participate with many pastors and teachers, but we found support in the fact that this was not our doing, God had a plan for us.

We learned a lot. For one thing, support-raising is essential to missionary preparation. Missionaries must raise the funds to finance their work abroad. The first step, we were told, was to make a slide presentation. We began praying about our newest challenge: showing others how God had led us up to this point. As we pondered all this in our hearts we realized the best place to start would be the beginning.

Dave's beginning was different than mine, but both our beginnings were a part of who we were now. We needed to put our beginnings together in a special way, so we began reflecting and writing about who we were.

As a child, Dave remembered little about church, although his family usually attended. It seemed to him that as his family grew in size (to five children), the family problems grew also and their attendance at church steadily declined. When Dave was 12, his parents divorced, and he went to church rarely, if at all. As many kids do when their parents break up, he started to look for ways to rebel. He fell in with the "tough guys" in school and got into quite a bit of mischief.

Looking back, Dave felt that God must have really been looking out for him, because some of his high school friends ended up in group homes or jail and some even died in alcohol or drug-related accidents. The Lord spared him from going through many of the trials and suffering that his friends went through.

While in high school, Dave worked part-time in a department store snack shop. It was over a coke and fries that we met. (I worked in another part of the store.) Dave said he always felt attracted to something I had inside of me; something he later found out was Christ. We began dating when I was sixteen and he was seventeen. Soon after I asked if he would like to go to church with me. The following Sunday we went to a church that had been planted by the church Dave had grown up in as a child and many people knew him. In fact, one man had been his Sunday School teacher about a dozen years before.

Dave started attending church, Sunday school, and youth group regularly. He was starting to know more about Jesus, but still did not know Jesus as his personal savior. Then one day he had a meaningful conversation with the pastor, who talked about Jesus, why He came to earth, and why He gave His life and shed His blood. He did it for us because He loved us. It was then that Dave recognized a real need in his life for Christ. He asked Jesus to forgive his sinfulness and asked Him to come into his heart. Not long after this, Dave and I were married in August of 1971.

For many years after receiving Christ as his personal Savior, Dave was content just knowing that when he died he would go to heaven. He taught Sunday school, helped with the Awana clubs, and even served on the church board, but he did not feel that he was really getting into God's word and praying like he should. After going through a period of not feeling well physically and not feeling good about himself he said to God, "Lord, I know I need to make some changes in my life. I need to get my priorities straight. Give me a desire to get into your Word daily and come to you in prayer daily." God answered that prayer and gave him a great hunger to get into His Word daily and come to Him daily in prayer.

One of the books that had been helpful in changing his thinking was the book of Ecclesiastes. Before our call to missions, Dave studied it, meditated on it and asked God what He had in this book for him. Solomon talks about his riches, his wisdom, his whole life and then Solomon said, "Meaningless, everything is meaningless." Dave looked at these verses and asked God, "Is everything I am doing in my life meaningless?" The Lord spoke to his heart and said, "Any part of your life that you are withholding from me and trying to do your way is going to be meaningless." Dave realized he was not letting God control all of his life. It was then that he asked God to take complete control of all of his life. He asked God to use him, wherever and whatever He wanted him to do or go, he would be His willing servant.

It seemed to Dave like more and more of the messages he heard from the pulpit, in the Bible and on the local Christian radio programs were about missions. The content of the sermons, radio programs and the Bible were not changing, he was. God was taking that earnest prayer and was starting to change him.

Now I would like to share my own beginnings. I grew up in a home where there was love, for which I thank the Lord. We had our problems, but the Lord carried us through them. I am sure I did not realize at the time just how much the Lord was taking care of us.

My dad was an alcoholic, but when he was not drinking you could not ask for a better father. My mother put up with so much from my father, yet you could always see (when he was not drinking) just how much they loved each other.

One incident in particular marked my life forever. I remember asking my mom, "How can you take so much and yet be so strong and still show Dad so much love?"

She said, "It is only because of the Lord. He gives me the strength." This made a tremendous impression on my life. I realized there is a God we can draw strength from and because of Him, my life had a stability I could not have otherwise had. This sounded like a loving God, one I would strive to know more about.

When I was about 12 years old I began seriously thinking about heaven and wondering if I would be good enough to go there. We went to Sunday school and church every Sunday. I would hear how I could have the assurance of going to heaven by accepting Jesus Christ as my Savior, but at that age I did not pay much attention in Sunday school.

One summer I went to Bible Camp and the Lord really spoke to my heart through the evangelist. I realized right then and there that I was a sinner and I wanted to make Jesus Lord of my life. I prayed and asked Jesus to forgive me of my sins and to come into my life. I finally received the assurance about heaven that I had been wanting. I knew I would someday be in heaven with Jesus. I was content knowing that and just went on my merry way, just as I had before I accepted Jesus.

A few years after my summer camp experience, our lives would take another turn. I was preparing to enter middle school when my dad announced that we would be moving again.

It seemed like the history of our family was to move about every three to four years, but I was not that excited about this move. I would be in my first year of middle school.

The time came for us to leave Illinois and move to Madison, Wisconsin. I was quickly enrolled in Schenk Junior High School. I went there for two years and then on to Lafollette High School.

While in high school I met a young man named, David Gove. He had a smile that melted my heart, but he was different than the usual boys I dated. He hung around with the wild crowd, but I could see that deep inside that was not who he really was. He was a nice quiet young man.

He finally asked me on a date and from that time on we were together all of the time.

In 1971 Dave and I were married. We were young, but I felt certain the Lord wanted us together. Before we were married Dave had accepted Jesus Christ as his personal Savior. At the time, we did not realize how important it was to read the Bible and to pray daily, which was the only way we would understand how to live as Christians.

Many years passed, and we were happy in our marriage. God blessed us with four beautiful, healthy sons. I remember after our second son was born thinking, "Maybe God is giving us sons to be used on a mission field someday." The thought came and went, and I did not think about it again for many years.

The next few years of our lives were challenging. I got to the point where I knew I was slipping away from God and I did not want that to happen. I came across the book *Lord, Change Me* by Evelyn Christensen and I read it.

In the book she challenged me to pray, "Lord, change me, not anyone else, just me." That was exactly what I needed at this point in my life. I prayed this and it was not long before things began to happen. Dave had an accident and ended up in the hospital. I had to depend on the Lord for physical strength and trust that He would provide for our needs. It was a trying time, but the Lord was right there with me. During this time I began reading my Bible and praying daily (for the strength I needed, just like my mom had said.) It was hard initially to find the time because satan would do everything in his power to prevent it. At times I would read the Bible and not really understand much. I would humbly get down on my knees and asked God to help me to understand it. Understanding God's word does not just happen. I realized that I needed to make a commitment to Him. I would keep studying and if God wanted me to understand, He would have to show me. As I began to make God a priority in my life, the Bible came alive to me and praying was something I began to long for. I knew He wanted this in my life for years, but my stubbornness did not allow time for Him. It was not until I faced trials in my life that I desired what God had been wanting for me since I became His child.

Meditating on God's word led me to many opportunities to enrich my life. It says in God's word “love one another” (I Peter 1:22). I thought about it and knew that I loved my family and close friends, but what about my neighbors and others? Did I really love others? Since this was something God wanted in my life, I knew that if I prayed about it, surely He would answer that prayer. I made this part of my prayer life and gradually noticed that I was changing. `I began to look at people differently. It was always so easy to look at the negative in others. I was learning to look at the positive because I truly believed that if I looked hard enough I could find it in anyone, with God's help. To this day it is a daily prayer of mine that God will put a love for others in my heart, because as a human being it is certainly not something I can acquire on my own.

It also says in God's word to "help others," (Hebrews 13:16). I thought, do I help others? Life is fast-paced and it is difficult to find time for all the needs in my own life, let alone others' needs. Prayer must be the only way, so I began to pray about this as well. It always amazes me when I see God answering a prayer in my life. It was not long before a woman came into my life that really needed my help. I had the choice to help her or go my own way. I knew this woman was an answer to my prayer. I began helping her with some of her various needs and to my surprise I realized how much I was enjoying it. It truly is more blessed to give than to receive.

One other important thing I was learning is that we were put on this earth for a good reason: to tell others how much God loved them. I was always afraid to share my faith in Jesus with others, so I began praying for the boldness and strength to do this. I had a deep concern for those who do not know Jesus as their Savior. God quickly answered my prayer. One Sunday our church bulletin announced an evangelism class. "Thanks, Lord," I prayed. I was excited about this class and was sure there would be a good turnout. I was wrong. Only three men were there the first night. I left feeling disappointed and apprehensive about practicing evangelism with men, as they do not think the same way as I do. I prayed and asked God for the strength and courage to make it through the class.

Every time class would roll around, I would have a bad day in anticipation of it. I am sure the devil was trying to discourage me so I would not feel like going to my class, but it says in 1 John 4:4, "Greater is He that is in me than He that is in the world." I never missed a class, even though it was hard work. We did a great deal of reading and memorizing of scripture, but I grew to love it.

Then came the night when we actually went out to people's homes. It was one of the hardest experiences I had ever been through. We would spend time praying in our class because we knew God would have to give us the courage and strength to do this.

After we prayed, we went out to various homes to share our stories of how we came to know God in our lives. I shared my story of my summer Bible Camp experience.

I would go home feeling so joyous, having shared about Jesus' love with someone new. This class was very important for me in my spiritual walk. It is not always easy to do what God leads us to do, but we can be assured He will be right there with us to hold us up and encourage us.

The deep desire in my heart was to share God's love with those in my world, but also with those who did not have opportunities to hear as we do. Doing missionary work was a burning desire in my heart. Would God fuel that fire?

Dave and I reflected on our beginnings from our childhood to where we were now. We put it all together in a slide presentation to share at churches. It was our biggest challenge, but the verse "all things are possible with God" encouraged us. With the slide presentation ready, we focused our attention on raising the needed support to get us on the field. We put our task in God's hands.

It was a difficult year, going from church to church, sharing our life. We felt committed to doing this as a family, so each weekend we would pack up our four children and off we would go to spend another night in a strange home. God's people always made us feel so welcome.

We would wait every day with anticipation for the mail. Maybe this would be the day we would receive word of new support. At times, we were so down we felt like giving up, but God would send us just the encouragement we needed to keep us going.

I remember one day feeling ready to call it quits. That day we received a letter in the mail from a church in Chicago saying they would be supporting us with a substantial amount. We had never even met anyone from this church, so this lifted our spirits and gave us the momentum to keep going.

Another time when we needed encouragement we received a letter from the Philippines telling us they were looking forward to us coming. They gave us specifics on what we would be doing when we arrived: helping the "career missionaries" in church planting in Manila. They also sent us a picture of where we would be living. We often looked at that picture, longing to be there.

It was a long year, but it was a year of growth in our lives. We learned to trust God in ways we never realized we could. We did not realize it at the time, but it was a period that would prepare us for what was in store for us. The year had made us stronger in every way and our faith had grown tremendously.

Chapter 3

THE JOURNEY BEGINS

Have I not commanded you? Be strong and courageous. Do not be terrified; do not be discouraged, for the Lord your God will go with you wherever you go.

Joshua 1:9

It was a crisp, sunny August day that we were officially commissioned as missionaries. The year was 1985. Excitement infused our lives as never before. The day had finally arrived. It seemed like only yesterday that we had stepped out in faith into this new venture. It had been a very long year filled with many challenges. Would we ever forget all that we had learned? I guess God allows those times in our lives so we will not forget, but learn from them.

As I gazed around the crowded room where everyone was gathered for our commissioning service, the reality of it all set in. We would soon be leaving the land of our birth, the land that we loved, to go halfway around the world to a country and people unknown to us. I realized more than ever that I could only go knowing that this was God's plan for us. God does have a special plan for each of His children. As we walk forward by faith He makes it clear what that plan might be. We knew without any doubt that we were following God's plan for us. In just a few short hours Dave and I would be boarding the plane with our four boys, soaring over the ends of the earth, entering into a new phase in God's plan for our lives.

The day before we departed for the Philippines we said our good-byes to family and friends. I had a constant lump in my throat and thought I would burst with emotion. As the sun set and the day drew to a close, even the darkness of the night could not stop the adrenaline from flowing in our veins. Sleep was not the order for this night, our last in the good old USA for at least for two years.

WHAT LIES AHEAD?

The day of our long-awaited journey arrived. Anxious thoughts were racing through my mind on our eighteen-hour flight: "What lies ahead? What will it be like living in a foreign country? Will the people be friendly? What about the other missionaries, how will we get along with them? What types of ministries will we be doing?" The answers to these and many other questions would soon begin to unfold.

To me, the most awesome sight in the world is to be so high that you float through the clouds and like a magnet we are attracted toward the glow of the sun. Looking down on the patchwork quilt of the earth, the greens of the fields, the browns of the earth, the blues of the rivers and oceans and the massive stone of the mountains with the peaks covered with the white of winter opened my eyes to the wonder of our Creator.

As our plane approached our destination, the black of the night was all around except for the twinkle of a star here and there, but suddenly the lights of Manila began to grow. Finally everywhere we looked was dotted with black and white. This was it; we had finally arrived.

Moving a family of six into a new life involves a lot of luggage. As we claimed our fourteen pieces, plus our six carry-ons and made our way through the airport, the smiles on the faces of those we met warmed our hearts. Customs in a country like this can be a real challenge, but we are quite sure the prayers of many allowed us to walk through customs without them looking at even one item.

The door to the outside world lay right before us. Who would meet us on the other side? We briskly continued on; the doors automatically opened and a rush of humid air engulfed us. We caught our breath, and as we looked up, a sign being held high in the air declared "Welcome Goves."

OUR NEW FAMILY

There they were—our family away from home. We were greeted in the Filipino way of placing a lei of aromatic flowers around each of our necks. The scent was heavenly.

After introductions were made, we were on our way to the place we would call home for the next two years. The ride was a rough one, as potholes jostled us and jeepneys (an extended jeep for transporting people) overflowing with people sped past us and left behind a wake of carbon monoxide. Our eyes soaked up all the sights on the way: the majestic palm trees gently blowing in the wind, the tall slender buildings of Manila were much like the sights of Chicago. This scene was offset by the winding rivers with small, frail inhabited shanties lining the edge, with trash floating in the water. The contrasts of rich and poor were evident everywhere.

Eventually we pulled onto a street with a small guard shack in the middle of it and to enter, a gate on either side had to be opened. A man wearing a dark blue uniform, fit snugly to his lean body, with a serious look on his clean-shaven face, approached the vehicle. Tied tightly to his side was a gun, which startled us for a minute before we realized this was for our own protection. He looked at us and our car closely to make sure it was all right to enter. In the months to come, these guards would become our friends. Gated subdivisions were quite common there.

Just inside the gate was our home, which would not only house us, but also three other families and our newly formed church. As I looked up at the massive building, it looked inviting. It reminded me of a huge square four-unit apartment building. Typical of the areas Spanish style, it had a rough texture and was painted a pale yellow with dark brown trim.

Feeling both exhausted and excited, we climbed the stairs into the sanctuary of our church. It was an enormous empty room, done in light oak paneling, wood slat floors, and one wall with a line of windows reaching high to the ceiling. The florescent lights beaming brightly made the room aglow.

"Welcome to the Philippines!" everyone shouted. Ice cream and more missionaries awaited our arrival. The fellowship we enjoyed that night was a treasure we would store in our hearts forever. Eventually, though, our exhaustion caught up with us, and we called it a night.

One of the doors off of this room led to our new home: a medium-sized living room, with the same oak paneling, lights, and windows, and off of that room, three small bedrooms, a small kitchen and a tiny bathroom at the end. We had now gone from a home with over two thousand square feet to an apartment with less than seven hundred square feet. It was small and cozy and we loved it.

We tried our best to relieve our exhaustion with sleep, but jet lag had confused our internal clocks. So in the late hours of this evening we began unpacking our bags, beginning to make this our home. The following week, jet lag really took its toll. We forced ourselves to stay awake during the day so we could begin to sleep at night. Various missionaries welcomed us into their homes, and after supper as our eyelids began to droop, they would try their best to keep us awake. When the task became impossible, they would say, "Time to head home!"

Our church house was brand new. It's purpose was to house as many people as possible, to help pay off the mortgage for the building with the tenants rent and then have an immediate church to meet in. We were fortunate to be one of the first groups to try out this concept and arrive at the early stages of church planting.

We did finally adjust to the time-change and the excitement of our new life began to grow. Our sons were enrolled in the local missionary kid's school, which was two kilometers from our house. Dave and I were enrolled in language school. I sure had a rough time catching on to this new language—Tagalog.

I will never forget our first day of language school. The older boys went off to school, but our youngest, Aaron, had to stay with our house-helper, Regie. He cried, "Mommy, I do not want you to go!" My heart ached as I left that morning. I had to trust God that He would be especially close to Aaron that day. As time went on he did adjust to me being in language school and grew to love his times with Regie.

Along with learning the language, we began getting to know the people who lived in our subdivision, which was a middle-class area. We would spend many hot humid evenings out walking up and down the streets of our subdivision. We began to know our neighbors. We even became brave enough to try Tagalog on them. They loved it when we would say, "Magadang Umaga, Po," which means "Good Morning, Sir or Ma'am." Or "Kumasta Ka," which means, "How are you?" It did not take us long to realize just how special the Filipino people were. They always had a smile to share with us.

DAILY LIVING

The houses in our area each had a tall brick wall with either broken glass or pointed hooks on top to keep unwelcome strangers out. Heavy iron gates crossed driveways and sidewalks. Inside the houses, the rooms were small and dark with marble floors that would keep the house cool in the high temperatures. Bathtubs were unusual. Often there would be two kitchens in one house, one a regular kitchen and the other a dirty kitchen outside where food was cleaned.

Our church house was near the entrance to the subdivision, so everyone within the subdivision began to know who we were and where we lived. Having Americans living within their walls was somewhat of a status symbol. Our children with their blonde hair became a novelty to people who passed and they would try and touch it just to see how it felt.

I know I also had the desire to touch the shiny, jet-black hair of the Filipinos to see if it felt as silky as it looked.

Also, at the entrance was the tricycle stand, where motorcycles with covered seats attached to the side would sit and wait for passengers. Most people who lived inside the gates did not have cars so in the morning they would take a brightly colored tricycle to the gate and then take a jeepney, a form of public transportation, to their work. Traffic was unbelievable, so we preferred public transportation. If you drove in the Philippines you were taking your life into your own hands.

We knew there would be times when we needed to drive, so one day Dave and I decided to go and get our licenses. It was a memorable day. It was hot and humid, as it always was and we waited in line with sweat rolling down our faces and our clothes sticking to our bodies. When the time came for us to get our licenses, the woman behind the counter looked us squarely in the eye and said, "You need a physical to get a license."

We asked, "Where could we get one?" She pointed to a man sitting a few feet away at a table.

Before we even spoke, the man looked at us and said, "30 pesos," and stamped a paper and handed it to us. We paid him the money. We looked down to see what we bought; it was a health status sheet saying we were perfectly healthy. Then he said, "Get back in line." We did and were given our licenses.

Eventually, I learned to drive just as crazy as everyone else. I had to so that I would survive, but before I could begin, I needed to learn some of the rules. One important rule is when you are approaching a car head-on and it wants to turn, the driver will flick his lights and take the right of way—without stopping. Another rule is if a driver beeps his horn he will proceed in whatever direction he wants, regardless of where other cars are. The rule of the road was; first one to flash the lights or honk the horn, has the right of way

One day I waited a very long time at a four-way stop. Cars were backed up for many blocks. It was Christmastime so traffic was heavier than usual, and people's nerves were more edgy. We moved inch by inch, as each vehicle would go through the intersection. Things do not work the same at intersections there as they do in the States. Whoever was the bravest went first. When my turn came, I was not the least bit bold. I waited and waited. My legs began to tremble as I tried to push the gas pedal, but nothing happened. Then I really believe God sent a little angel for me.

A jeepney driver stopped his jeep, got out, went into the middle of the intersection, stopped the traffic and waved me by. I praised God!

THE OPEN MARKET

Grocery shopping was another learning experience. Open markets were the general means of shopping for meats, vegetables, and fruits. When I say "open," I mean it. We could see beef freshly butchered and hanging by a hook from the top of the stand. Some of our favorites to look at—but not eat—were pig heads. You could look at a row of pig heads and take your pick. We once went to the market for a chicken, we picked out one and they butchered it right there for us. Fish of all kinds would be laying flat, side-by-side, for you to choose. I often wondered why Americans are so set on refrigeration, because all of this meat would withstand the high temperatures and humidity and still look fresh and appetizing. The odors of the market were sometimes pungent, but we never tasted any spoiled meat. Eggs were another item that was never refrigerated. We could buy them right off of the shelf. This took some getting used to, but we managed.

The vegetables and fruit were magnificent—an amazing variety of each. It made our suppers a real feast. Our favorite fruit was mangoes. The first time we had them we did not like them, but it soon turned into love.

Besides the open market, there were typical grocery stores,

usually dark, probably to keep the heat out. It did not have the rows and rows of cereal and dog food like in the States, but it did carry much of what we needed. If they did not have what we wanted we could buy just about any item from the States on the local black market—for a price, of course.

We learned to enjoy a lot of the Philippine food, like lumpia, which was much like an egg roll. Bucco salad, which is baby coconut grated up with a lot of cream and pineapple, became my favorite. Rice, of course, was the staple of our diet. Once Dave was served dog meat, which he ate. Luckily, I was not with him when he enjoyed that delicacy. Another family favorite was chicken and pork adobo. We did miss some of our favorites like homemade pizza, ham, and turkey, but we enjoyed experiencing another country's cultural foods.

One day I had some ladies over for lunch. They had decided that they knew me well enough to treat me to a dish they served only to family. I was wise enough not to ask what it was until I tasted it. It was brown-colored and resembled lumpy chocolate pudding served over rice. I thought it would be sweet, but it was not. Well, I found out later it was—are you ready for this?—blood and intestines. Needless to say, the leftovers were not eaten.

Adjusting to our new country had its challenges, but we could feel the prayers of our family and friends and had the sense that we were doing great. More challenges, however, were soon to come.

Chapter 4

GOD IS FAITHFUL

Have faith in the Lord your God and you will be upheld.

2 Chronicles 20:20b

Do the trials and tribulations in our lives allow us to trust God more? Does our faith grow stronger with each passing day? It is the fiery circumstances in our lives, the times of not really knowing which way to turn, where we learn to trust God more. My family would soon go through one of those fiery trials. Would our faith grow?

EMOTIONAL SUPPORT

A few months into our missionary commitment, David, our oldest son who was thirteen years old at the time, began to experience an inner conflict. We did not become aware of it until the day it boiled over.

"I want to leave this place! I do not like it here! I'll take a jeepney to the airport and go home!" David cried out. The words tore through my heart as nothing else could. Parents who see their children hurting will do anything in their power to help relieve the pain. What could we do? Had we made a mistake coming here? Could we possibly continue in something that was hurting our son? After searching our souls for the answer, we realized there was nothing we could do but *pray* and trust God. We began telling as many people as we could, "Please pray for

David, he is hurting."

Our faith was being tested in a way we had never experienced before. We gave the situation totally to God because we were helpless to change anything. God would have to change David's heart. We prayed, "God, you have called us here for a purpose. We desire more than anything to do your will, but our son is hurting. We realize you are the only answer. We will be trusting you to take care of him."

A miracle happened: David began playing basketball with the neighborhood Filipino boys. He started attending our newly formed church youth group, which was totally in Tagalog. He asked our house-helper to talk to him in her language. He started speaking Tagalog fluently and impressed the Filipinos. They would say, "David really speaks our language well."

God indeed provided a miracle in our son's life. A love grew in his heart, for this country and its' people, to the point he did not want to go back home.

God always knew what we needed before we did ourselves. One of the greatest ways he encouraged us was by sending family and friends to visit us. You will never really understand how it feels to have someone from home come to visit unless you experience it first-hand. We were overwhelmed with joy when we realized that my mom (Adeline) and my step-dad (Lloyd) would be coming to visit us. We counted the days to their arrival.

They finally arrived. We wanted to show them as many things as we could during their visit. The tour began with our church and ministry in our subdivision, Vista Verde. Then we took them to downtown Manila showing them the ruins from World War II. My step-dad had actually been in the Philippines during the war, so it brought back many memories for him. We took a little trip to a resort where we could see what the provinces (or country) of the Philippines were like. We visited a very unique restaurant in an area called Makati. It had a beautiful new Jeepney that had a table inside of it where we enjoyed a wonderful meal.

We had a lot of fun together. It was so great to see them. I am not sure they ever realized what an encouragement they were to us. We were so blessed to have them come and visit.

We also had friends visit us for the weekend. Howard and Carol Wilson were another special blessing from God. Howard worked for the airlines and was able to fly standby to visit us for the weekend. I am not sure how they even stayed awake for the weekend with jetlag, but the time we spent with them was priceless.

Yes, God knows what we need and when we need it. We can trust that He will send us what we need to keep us going in whatever challenges we face in our lives.

MATERIAL SUPPORT

Over and over we learned to trust God with our daily needs and challenges. Living on a missionary's salary was one of our biggest hurdles to overcome. The roughly $12,000 in annual salary quickly went for rent, food, clothes and supplies. We learned the difference between necessities and luxuries. God really did provide both, but so often we were powerless. The money would disappear quickly, but God would provide in some unbelievable way.

Once our son Aaron's shoes had holes in them, but the money was gone. Charge cards were not an option. The next day, after we had prayed specifically about it, an unexpected check from a dear friend arrived in the mail. God knows what we need more than we do ourselves. He is always faithful.

We lived the first year without a television. We did miss watching a good show once in awhile and also the news. We could not afford to buy a TV so we prayed, "God, if it is your will, provide us with this luxury. If not, that is okay, too." A few weeks later a woman who had been coming to our church visited our home. She looked around the room with a puzzled look on her face. She questioned, "Do you have a television?" Of course our reply was no. She asked us,

"Why not?" We explained that we did not feel we could afford one. She replied, "I have an extra one. Would you like to use it until you can get one yourself?" That very night excitement filled the room as we watched the news on our television. Most of the programs were in Tagalog, but that helped us learn the language.

PHYSICAL SUPPORT

What about our physical needs? Will God provide?

Dave and I had been working incredibly hard doing our language studies, leading Bible studies, developing planning committees, and also attending staff meetings. We also spent a lot of time helping with the physical needs of many. Through all our busyness we did not realize it, but our own bodies were beginning to wear down. We needed to get away to gain physical strength and rest.

How could we ever do that with all of our responsibilities? We prayed, "God, you know we need some rest. Please provide so we can get away for a weekend. Most importantly, Lord, we would need someone to stay with the kids. Someone we could trust."

It was not long before we received one hundred dollars in the mail from friends back home to do something fun. Thinking it over we decided there was only one person we felt we could ask to stay with our boys. We asked our friend, Arlys, and her reply was, "I would love to!"

Dave and I were soon relaxing at a beautiful resort, just the two of us. We spent the whole weekend sleeping and eating, but that is what our bodies needed. We returned home refreshed, praising God for His provisions.

SPIRITUAL SUPPORT

God is faithful. When He calls us to do something He gives us what we need to accomplish it. We understood that the only way we could ever have any ministry at all was due to the power of God working in us. By ourselves, we are so unqualified, but with God all things are possible.

The Filipino pastor of our church asked my husband if he would be willing to preach in church one Sunday. Dave had only preached a few times throughout our missions' journey so he lacked full confidence in his abilities. He knew that he could not do it on his own. He trusted that God would help him do this, so he accepted the challenge. The night before he was supposed to preach he came down with the flu. He wondered if he should just ask the pastor to fill in, but instead he told the Lord, "God, not only am I not qualified to preach, but now I am physically unable to do it on my own. You will have to take control."

The next morning Dave stood before a congregation of fifty people and preached a message God had laid on his heart. The words spoke to my heart in a tremendous way. After the service, people told him, "Dave, you are a gifted speaker. You must preach more often." In fact, he began preaching once a month. He learned what it meant to give God total control and God blessed him for it.

PHILIPPINE REVOLUTION

One of our biggest "faith builders" came just five months after we arrived in Manila when the Philippine revolution erupted. The presidential election results had been corrupted and tension filled the city. Everywhere we would go radios and televisions would be blaring as people listened intently to the latest news. Juan Ponce Enrile, the Minister of National Defense, firmly said, "The election was a fraud! I can no longer work under the present leadership."

The snap election between Ferdanand Marcos and Cory Aquino was the dirtiest in Philippine history, according to many. Riots and protests were brewing everywhere. Many registered voters' names could not be found.

Marcos claimed, "I have won this election!" Aquino's words were the same. I wondered, "What should the people believe?" Who was their leader? Confusion, frustration, and anger burned in the hearts of the people.

Meanwhile our mission leaders said, "We have never seen this country in so much turmoil. It looks like a revolution will soon be upon us. Our safety might be threatened. We want everyone to pack and be ready to evacuate in a moments notice." This was the last thing we wanted, since we had just arrived and God had called us here. Would we be willing to die if things grew worse?

The conflict grew as two prominent leaders rose to topple the present administration. Their commitment to change the turmoil in the country was contagious. People began gathering to show their support, but Marcos would not be shaken. He claimed victory and ordered an all-out attack. People filled the streets and marched around the palace. Something had to give and it did not look like it was going to be Ferdinand Marcos.

Subsequent coup attempts would cause the sky to be filled with mushroom clouds of smoke hovering over the horizon. From our church house, we had the experience of seeing planes dropping bombs on a nearby military camp. The loud rumbling noise of the bombs hitting their targets sent chills through my body. The buzzing sound of the fighter airplanes overhead caused us to fall to our knees in prayer.

Marcos finally fled the country. The tension dispersed and a feeling of victory took its place. The people had worked together for their country. They called it "people power." Those in our church agreed it was actually "prayer power."

We thank God for allowing us to experience the Philippine revolution and subsequent coup attempts. It again shows us how faithful our God is. We do not need to fret and worry when life hurls trials across our path. God is in control. He has a plan for us all. He will take care of us.

Chapter 5

PRAYER POWER

Pray continually; give thanks in all circumstances, for this is God's will for you in Christ Jesus.
I Thessalonians 5:17,18

In a missionary's life, the joy and excitement of serving God can become squelched by the trials of daily living and the constant demands on your time. Each moment becomes precious. If a missionary's priorities are not kept in line, satan will sneak up and snatch away time with the Lord. It is his goal to break our fellowship with our Lord and to take us over little by little. Our time in the Philippines was an incredible challenge and opportunity for growth for me in this respect.

While living in the States, I treasured my quiet time with the Lord. In fact, it was the high point of my day. Soon after arriving in the Philippines, I realized that my quiet time with the Lord was diminishing, as was my joy. My attitudes and actions were changing. I felt satan constantly knocking at my door. I realized, as I look back, why he was attacking me. I had given him a foothold in my life, and I would like to share what that foothold was.

SATAN'S FOOTHOLD

For many people, satan's foothold can be something that seems deceptively simple. I have always prayed that God would give me a gentle, quiet spirit. He has shown me repeatedly that for me to have a gentle, quiet spirit I need to steer clear of caffeine in soda drinks and sugar or at least find more of a balance with it. When I eat or drink them I become irritable. My personality changes completely. They affect me physically, emotionally, and spiritually. I am not saying that it is bad for everyone, but I know it is for me.

With God's help I had victory over this hurdle while in the States, but when I arrived in the Philippines sugar was inescapable. In many areas you could not drink the water because it was unsafe, so soda was a safe alternative. Milk and pineapple juices were healthy choices, but you could not get them everywhere. It was a constant battle for me. I would hear that little voice inside say, "No," but it was so hard to listen. I know it affected me spiritually because whenever I had too much soda drinks and sugar I felt I was disobeying God. In I Corinthians 3:16,17 it says, "Do not you know that you yourselves are God's temple and that God's spirit lives in you? If anyone destroys God's temple, God will destroy him, for God's temple is sacred, and you are that temple." I was hurting my body by the things I ate and drank. I would rationalize every way I could in my mind each time I would disobey. I would think, "Everybody in the world eats sugar and drink soda!" Then I would think, "Yes, and many people do drugs and drink alcohol. Does that make it right for me?"

I felt that sin in my life was keeping my fellowship with God from being what it ought to be. As a result my whole person, attitudes, and actions were affected. So what did God do? He made me realize I must allow Him to help me to find balance in my life and get right with Him. I resolved again to avoid this temptation so my body and emotions were sound.

QUIET TIME

I also realized that if I wanted to have a quiet time with God it needed to be early in the morning or else the day would pass by. One day I prayed, "God, if you want me to get up early and study, show me." Then one morning I woke up at 4:00 a.m. and thought, "Lord, you do not mean for me to get up now, do you?" Well, I could not get back to sleep. That little voice inside kept saying, "Get up!" I finally did, and for two hours I enjoyed studying, spending time in God's word, and praying. I began to wake up every morning at this same time. I felt God had allowed me to wake up this early because it was the only way I would spend time with Him. It was hard at first, but it then became a habit.

I soon saw that even one day without the Lord would give the devil a foothold. I had never experienced the power of satan as much as I did on the mission field. When we were out sharing the word of God, satan would do everything in his power to keep us from being obedient to what God had called us to do. I praise God for showing me that He is the only one who could help me to overcome satan's power in those days.

After I began spending time with the Lord early in the morning, my quiet time with Him blossomed. I would begin my times together by asking God to forgive me for anything I might have done that would not please Him. Sin in my life would hinder our communication. I did not want that to happen. I would ask God, "How do you want me to change?" He revealed to me many things that He wanted changed in my life. I knew I could not change on my own, but only with God's power and His patience and guidance could I change. I asked, "Lord, I know I am a missionary in the Philippines, but am I doing all that you would have me to do? Your word tells us to be a servant. Teach me what that means." All my life I have been a leader, but I longed to understand what being a servant meant. That was my prayer—to have a "servant's attitude." Sometimes it seems that extroverted people find it hard to be a servant, but Jesus was a servant. He is our example and no matter how hard it would be, that is what I wanted. We might not always agree with our earthly masters, but God has put them where they are, and we must obey.

PRAYER LIFE

I had been leading four Bible studies, which I truly enjoyed, but slowing they were all coming to an end. I wondered what I should do next. I began to pray about this, but that little voice inside of me kept repeating, "Just be still and listen." Being still is difficult for me, but I felt this is what I was supposed to do, so for several months I tried to listen to what that little voice was trying to teach me.

I felt like I was being prepared for something, but I did not know what. I continued studying and praying daily. I then began writing about all that I was learning. It was slowly developing into a seminar. I began to work on it everyday.

Then one day, I attended a team meeting. After it was over, I went about doing things I wanted to do, but that little voice within said, "Work on the seminar!" My response was, "I have worked on it for two hours already today, and I have other things to do." As I went about doing other things, peace was missing. I finally gave up and walked slowly to my desk and hesitantly sat down.

I picked up my pen and started writing. One by one ideas popped into my head. Before long, topics for three sessions came to my mind. I wrote them all down. As the weeks and months passed, I continued writing and learning. The seminar blossomed into three distinct sessions. The first one was about Prayer, the second one was about God speaking to us in Scripture and then the last one was about our relationships, first with God, then others. I began to realize I was living all that I was learning. The hardest part came when I had to learn first - hand how to mend a broken relationship.

BROKEN RELATIONSHIPS

I never had experienced a bad relationship before, but God had some important lessons to teach me. How else would I learn about the process of mending a bad relationship except by experiencing one?

Living in a church house was one of the hardest experiences and biggest adjustments I would ever make. Living together, working together, and socializing together with the same people and even people from different cultures is especially hard. What made it harder is that most Filipinos do not have the luxuries Americans do, which can lead to feelings of inequality—feelings that are not from God. Conditions like these can be a breeding ground for satan to work and create bad relationships.

There is no relationship that God cannot mend. I wanted to give up on a relationship with a fellow missionary, but that still, small voice would clearly say, "Have I given up on you?" Praise God He has not given up on me! I could not give up on this bad relationship either, but it would take hard work to mend it.

In any relationship we can look too closely at little things a person does—things we do not agree with. These little things can pile up and fester. Soon all we can see is the negative. That causes us to become critical. Judgment starts out small, but slowly it covers up all the good we once saw in a person. Matthew 7:5 says, "You hypocrite, first take the plank out of your own eye and then you will see clearly to remove the speck from your brother's eye." The only one I am accountable for is myself.

It is hard to swallow your pride and be the first one to try and make a relationship better. Proverbs 16:18 says, "Pride goes before destruction." We cannot do it on our own, but God is with us. If we pray about it, He will give us the words and the courage to do it. It is hard to say I am sorry, forgive me, even when you do not feel you are wrong. Philippians 4:13, says "I can do all things through Christ who gives me the strength." When you have a bad feeling for someone, the best way to overcome it is to say in your heart, "Yes. Lord, I forgive them" and really mean it.

I am thankful that God did not give up on me. He took me through a once-beautiful relationship and then allowed our sin to make it a relationship that was so bad I never thought it could be healed, but with God's power and love, He transformed it once again into a beautiful relationship.

God speaks to our hearts and guides us. I soon would understand more clearly another way that God would speak to me. Would I listen?

Chapter 6

SCRIPTURE POWER

For the word of God is living and active. Sharper than any double-edged sword, it penetrates even to dividing soul and spirit, joints and marrow; it judges the thoughts and attitudes of the heart.

Hebrews 4:12

In my morning writing sessions, there was a recurring theme. "How does God speak?" Of course, as Christians we know He speaks through His word and also through His Holy Spirit in our hearts. I wondered, "How much listening do I do, I mean truly listening to God, expecting Him to speak?" There was a deep longing in my heart to know the answers. Because I knew that only God could give me understanding, I began earnestly praying, "God, please give me a discerning heart when you speak. As I race through life, give me the desire to stop the race and listen and the hardest part, OBEY."

PLEASE CHANGE ME, LORD

I sincerely wanted to see clearly what God wanted me to do or change in my life. Many years prior I prayed, "*Lord, Change Me,*" as suggested in a book by Evelyn Christiansen. God had taken that prayer and began working in my life and believe me, it hurt. Many trials came rushing in on me. I felt overwhelmed with my life and wondered where God was. It got to the point that I did not even feel like praying. I felt as though my heart was turning cold towards God, but what could I do about it? Then I heard about a Bible study that was close to my home. I decided to try it out. It was wonderful and joy slowly returned to my life.

So here I was again, contemplating praying again that God would change me. Who would ever pray for something if you knew it would cause pain? I tried to avoid thinking about changing, but that still, small voice kept speaking louder and louder. My peace had disappeared, telling me that this was what God wanted in my life. A willingness to allow God to change me, not anyone else in my life, just me was the reality I was running from.

Finally, I could not run any longer. I said to the Lord, "Change me and if it hurts, be there to pick me up in your loving arms and carry me through." The book *Lord, Change Me* mentioned reading God's word until He speaks. I wondered what this meant. I longed to clearly hear the voice of God in everything I do and say. I truly desired to OBEY. I once asked a wise person, "How do you know whether the voice we hear is from God, satan, or me?" The reply was, "The more time you spend with someone, the sooner you recognize their voice." So I began reading God's word and waiting for Him to speak.

I began by asking God, "Please speak to me." Then I would pick up the Bible and read a portion of scripture. Without fail, a verse would pop out at me. If I would keep reading past it, that same verse would come to my mind. When God would speak, I would immediately stop and listen, otherwise satan would quietly creep in and confuse me.

My heart was touched the first time I tried this. Tears of joy flowed down my cheeks. I had been stopped at a verse that was relevant for what I was going through in my life.

I began to expand on this idea and I would begin reading starting with Galatians 5:1. I would read until a verse touched my heart and then I would stop and think about what this verse was saying to me. I would write my thoughts down and then I would do the same thing beginning in Ephesians 1:1, Philippians 1:1 and Colossians 3:1. I was amazed to see a pattern emerging. God would speak to my heart about a need or sin in my life in Galatians and Ephesians and then in Philippians and Colossians go on to speak about what I needed to do about it. I was so excited to see what was happening.

I would get up very early every morning and spend time doing this. The words of the Bible spoke to me very clearly. It truly amazed me how the verses would speak to me about something that was going on in my life.

The word of God is living and active. It does not matter how many times you read it because each time you will learn something new and fresh. God wants to speak to us if we only take the time to listen.

I grew to love my times reading God's Word until it would speak to me. I actually looked forward to it. Thinking back on my life it is hard to imagine that there was a time when I never read the Bible. What made the difference? I believe the difference happened when I made God a priority in my life. I carved time out of my busy day because I understood the difference it made in my life.

Yes, there is POWER in the word of God. Scripture power continues to be a source of strength for my life.

Chapter 7

PEOPLE POWER

Ah, Sovereign Lord, you have made the heavens and the earth by your great power and outstretched arm. Nothing is too hard for you.

Jeremiah 32:17

During the Philippine revolution, "people power" was spoken about as the tool of victory. In our world today, God's power working together with "people power" can be our tool of victory over the sin that struggles to control the world.

I often wondered if I was doing my part to change this world. Alone, I could do little, but I learned that with many working together, much more could be accomplished. That is the key - working together!

WORKING TOGETHER

However, as I soon found out, working together brings many challenges. After all, most people who make it to the mission field have at least one person in each household who would be considered strong-willed. Getting those strong wills together could lead to a clash of wills, and it did many times.

There was a missionary woman who lived in our church house. She and I were very strong willed women. We thought differently about everything, and our wills began to clash. Often times it was over little things that happened, but we could blow it all out of proportion.

I made a discovery one day that upset me. We both had four children, but they had a dryer and we did not. Our house-helper would wash our clothes and let them dry out in the hot humid air all day. I did not have a problem with that until we realized that we were paying for the electricity for their dryer. We were not allowed to use it, but we paid for it. When we confronted them with it, they replied, "There's nothing we can do about it."

The anger raged within me. That still, small voice would try to direct my actions. It was hard. God was the only one who could control my emotions.

Many times in our relationship I would think, "It is not my fault! Why do I always have to be the one to make amends?" The battle continued, day and night. Outwardly we would speak pleasantly, but the undertones said, "I do not like you!" Before long, I found myself avoiding this woman altogether.

Then one day, while walking briskly through our neighborhood, I began thinking about this woman and our relationship. I thought, "God does not give up on me. Is it right for me to give up on this relationship?" Then that voice inside seemed to say, "Ask her to be in a Bible study with you!" My immediate reply was, "Absolutely, NO WAY!" As I thought about it, I knew only God could mend this relationship, but I wondered if I was willing to do all the work it would take.

Weeks passed and that voice inside of me kept prodding, "Ask her, ask her," but I was not willing to listen. The lack of peace in my life was slowly wearing me down, but I would not submit. I have come to realize if you run away from what God wants you to do, it won't be a pleasant experience. You cannot forget it. It is there day and night. Once I finally submit, the joy and peace flows immediately back into my life.

I could not take it anymore, so finally one day I blurted out almost in anger, "Okay, I will do it Lord, but she will say no and then it will not be my problem anymore." The next day I prayed for God to give me courage to ask her. I could not do it on my own!" I was almost hoping I would not see her, but before long I stood face to face with her. My body trembled inside as I asked her to start a Bible study with me. I waited anxiously for her reply so I could quickly leave. "Oh, that would be so nice," she replied in her gruff, stern way. I was shocked. This truly must be God's will for our relationship.

That night as I rested my head on my pillow I wondered what would have happened if I had never obeyed? I was happy and scared all at once. I prayed, "God, this whole thing is in your hands. Thank you for what you are going to do!" We began meeting once a week. It was awkward at first, but slowly the anger faded. As we would pray together God began to fill us with a love *for each other*. I suddenly saw that this woman had been on the mission field many years and was very lonely. I, on the other hand, was fresh and new and wanted to change everything I saw. God needed to teach us both how He wanted to change us.

The day came for this woman to return home to the States. I wrapped my arms around her as she squeezed hers around me. One lonely tear trickled down my face as I whispered in her ear, "I love you!" I know I really meant those words. I praised God for taking yet another bad relationship and making it something beautiful.

If we let Him, God can change any relationship. It might take days, weeks, months or even years, but as long as we obey His direction, victory will be ours. It is not always easy, but with God nothing is impossible.

Why does God allow us to go through the trying experiences we do? This is something I have questioned many times, but when we experience God's definite hand working as we did in this relationship, it gives us the strength to press on because in the end God will bless us when we obey what He is telling us to do.

HEAVENLY SOUP

In our world, wherever we are, we need to mend relationships and work together so God's power working with people power (the Filipino way to describe how people worked together during the revolution in their country) will take us one step closer to changing our world. Think of it as a recipe for "Heavenly soup." God is the maker of the soup. He puts different ingredients into the soup and they each have their own flavor. Some of the ingredients are riper than others and try to assert their flavors onto all the other ones, or maybe some are fresher than others, which can add freshness to the soup. Some of the ingredients may think, "Well, that ingredient is not very good because it is only going to be in the soup for a little while," or some just do not want to be in the soup anymore. Sometimes the ingredients just do not mix well together and the soup becomes sour. God is the chief cook and He has put all the ingredients in the soup and each ingredient is needed to make the soup the most delicious. So God keeps stirring the soup to make each ingredient the best taste it can be. The more God works on the soup the more the ingredients will blend together to make the soup delicious. When all the flavors begin to mingle and see the good in each of the other ingredients, eventually the soup can become a recipe made in heaven.

Will we let God stir us, or will we fall off the side of the pan, or cling to the spoon? Will we listen when God begins stirring and then obey, or will we cling to our own desires and thus sour the soup?

Learning to listen to that still, small voice within was God stirring me. It was hard. I wanted to jump out of the pan. I did not like the things that occurred. It was not until I submitted and listened and let God stir me, that I could see the good in the other ingredients in my soup.

Chapter 8

FOLLOWING GOD'S LEAD

Whether you turn to the right or to the left, your ears will hear a voice behind you, saying, "This is the way; walk in it."
Isaiah 30:21

One muggy day in the summer of 1988, I sat dreaming about our future. What began as two years of missionary work in the Philippines had turned into three. Soon our time here would come to a close. I wondered where we would go next. Would we return here after a furlough or stay back in the States for good? I knew that my desire was to return to the Philippines, but would that be God's plan?

I finally said to my husband, "Wouldn't it be nice to know where God wants us before we leave?"

He wisely replied, "Oh, I do not know, maybe it would be best to just wait until we get back to the States before we decide."

The strong will in me, fueled by my own desire, kept me from heeding my husband's advice. I continued to pray while I unknowingly proceeded in the direction of my desires.

My husband saw the reality of the situation: to return as career missionaries would mean raising a lot more support. He would also have to attend college for a few years and we had no clue where the money would come from. My faith kept telling me nothing is impossible with God.

One morning as Dave and I sat having breakfast at our favorite early morning coffeehouse, we talked about our future. He said, "I really enjoyed our time here. I know I will miss it, but I really do not want to be in the role of pastor the rest of my life."

I know my face could not hide the disappointment I felt for giving up the life we were now living. I quickly searched for a reason to return and said, "How would you feel about becoming the business manager for the mission? Do you think you would like that?"

"I am not sure," was his reply.

As time passed, Dave was asked to return to the Philippines and become the business manager of the mission. This was an answer to my prayers, or so I thought. They also agreed, due to the fact that our son wanted to finish his high school years at Faith Academy, where he had been attending, that we could go back to the States for the summer. We could visit relatives and friends and sell our house. Then we could return at the end of the summer and pick up where we left off.

The biggest question was if more schooling would be required of us. We were thrilled when they said that practical experience was worth more than all the education anyone could have. Everything was falling into place. The decision was made. We would go back to the States for the summer and then return in the fall. The kids were thrilled.

While we prepared to go home, we realized that the one important thing we would need as soon as we got home would be a car or van. We would be on the road all summer trying to raise more support so we needed something dependable. We asked God to provide for us. We believed that He would. Not long after, we received a letter from some dear friends, who wrote, "We know you will need something to drive when you arrive at home so we would like to offer our new van for you to drive." I was shocked and overwhelmed. We praised and thanked God again for His provision.

The time came to leave the Philippines. After a long flight we arrived back in the good old USA. Our friends, Bill and Carol, greeted us at the airport with their beautiful blue van with shiny silver trim—our

Cinderella pumpkin chariot. It was more than we could have ever dreamed of. Would you ever believe that people could be so unselfish and loving to allow their friends to use something of such great value for three whole months? It warmed our hearts as nothing could. We will always be grateful to our dear friends, Bill and Carol Wagner, for their gracious gift to us.

Our next order of business was deciding where to live. We had rented our house with an option to buy before leaving for the Philippines. In the days that followed, we found out that the people who were living in our house just left. Our house was a mess, but it was empty. We started the awesome task of cleaning and painting our house so we could live in it again. It felt good the day we moved into our own home again. We did not have any furniture because we sold it all before we left, but God is faithful. Some wonderful people from our church gave us odds and ends to use and soon our house felt like home.

ON THE ROAD AGAIN

We needed to achieve two goals in order to return to the Philippines: sell our home, and visit all our supporting churches to raise any additional support that we could. We quickly set about to this task. First we listed our home. Then we prepared a presentation in which we could share all that we had been doing while in the Philippines. Everything was prepared to begin our summer journey.

Our theme song for every weekend was "On The Road Again." Each Friday, we would pack the same things and head out to our next church on our journey. For me, I thrived on this and enjoyed it immensely, but for Dave and the kids, it was tiring.

June and July came and went. We had visited all of our churches, but we did not have all the support we needed. August arrived and nothing was happening. Our home had not sold. We realized that there was no way we could leave by the end of the summer, as our two goals had not been met. One or the other had to happen. If our house sold and our support did not come in, we would support ourselves.

WHAT IS GOD'S WILL?

At the end of summer, I took a blanket, my Bible and study books and walked to the back of our five-acre property. The sun was shining brightly in the early morning hours. I spread the blanket on the hot dry ground, sat down and poured my heart out to God. "Please show us what you want us to do. Nothing seems to be happening to allow for our return to the Philippines."

Then without warning that little voice inside seemed to reply, "Maybe going back to the Philippines is not God's will, but Robin's will!" I was stunned at the thought and tried to erase it, but it would not leave.

I finally confessed, "If that is true God, forgive me. Could I have manipulated everything, without knowing, because I longed to return to the Philippines? Please show me." I ended my quiet time that day with a huge hole in my heart. Before I made my way back to the house, a thought popped into my mind. I should have listened to my husband's wise advice back in the Philippines. He had suggested we wait until we get back to the States before we decide our future.

I was powerless, so I gave it to the Lord. "If it is your will God, that we stay back in the States, please work in Dave's heart to make him willing," I humbly pleaded. "You know when Dave makes a decision, he does not like to go back on it."

No change happened in our situation as the summer drew to a close. Because we were supposed to return the end of the summer and did not, our short-term salary would end until we returned. Dave had to find work.

He went to the company he worked for before we left and asked for work. They replied that they would really like a commitment that he would stay with them. "I cannot do that," was his reply. "We will be going back to the Philippines as soon as our house sells or our support comes in." Without hesitation they said, "When can you start?" He began working the very next day.

Labor Day came and went. Halloween and Thanksgiving did the same. No change! Then a week before Christmas we accepted an offer on the house. We had the papers all drawn up and were waiting for the man to come and sign them, but he did not come. We soon learned that he had been in a head-on collision that had killed someone. He was in the hospital in critical condition. When we thought our house was sold we began making plans in our mind about our return to the Philippines. Now we questioned, "God, do you want us to go back?"

As we waited for this man to heal, we received word from two of our supporters that they would have to quit supporting us until we returned. All of our money from supporters was put together in an account to be used when we left. This news was very discouraging.

GOD WAS SAYING NO!

We began to question if God was saying, "No," to our return. We struggled to face that fact. My heart ached realizing that God was closing the door for our return to the Philippines. The day we called the mission to tell them the news was the hardest day I have ever experienced. I cried until my body ached. I had to give up my dream.

"Where do you want us Lord? What do you want us doing? Do you really want us to stay right where we are?"

Chapter 9

THE LONELY DESERT

Remember how the Lord your God led you all the way in the desert these forty years, to humble you and to test you in order to know what was in your heart, whether or not you would keep His commands.
Deuteronomy 8:2

Winter came and went as I waited for God's plan for our family to become clear. One day I stood at our window, gazing at the beauty of the countryside. God's creation was evident everywhere, the rolling hillsides speckled with farm animals grazing, with splashes of white where the remains of winter had not yet left us. As I stood there, my soul was searching for answers. I never realized what was in store for me on this day. God would lovingly give me what I wanted more than anything. Would it be a blessing?

For years I had a yearning in my heart for what I dreamed my life to be. We all have dreams and goals, but I have learned that if these dreams and goals are not in God's plan, the pleasure of attaining them is missing. It took heartache in my life to make me willing to give up my desires and go with what God's desires were for me. Until those lessons were learned I clung to my dreams.

As a child growing up we moved quite often, which I loved. I thrived on starting fresh—moving to a different house, starting a new school and making new friends. So naturally, my life's dream did not include staying in the same place for the rest of my life. It also did not include snow. Most of my childhood days were spent in climates that included snow and at the time, I enjoyed the peacefulness and beauty of the first snowfall, the fun of making snow angels. I also recall riding in the car during the long, treacherous trip on slippery, snow-covered roads to my grandmother's house. The snow in Upper Michigan would be so high that they would have to build a deck from the porch to the street so you could get out. However, the older I got the less I liked the cold winter, so my dream included spending less time in it.

Another aspect of my dream was city life. I have always adored the lights and action of the big cities. While living in Manila, I remember many times driving high up into the mountains and seeing the night air hover mysteriously over the city. I felt awe-struck looking down at the lights of a city of ten million people. Just witnessing it would send a chill throughout my whole being. Of course, I needed my dream house in that big city. I envisioned an elegant, contemporary home, complete with an in-ground swimming pool, because from the time I was little I loved to swim and loved the water. I wanted a yard landscaped to perfection, giving total seclusion from everyone.

My dream revolved around being a wife and mother, which is all I really ever wanted out of life. I grew up with three older sisters, which was wonderful, but I always thought having a brother would be so exciting. Since that never happened, having sons was the ultimate blessing for me.

The idea of getting ahead in the work world was not a priority for me. My leadership abilities were dormant much of the time, so I projected this desire onto my husband. Yes, he would one day be in management, climbing the corporate ladder and leading his company to great success. As years passed I wondered if that was my husband's dream, as well, or would my encouragement in that direction lead us down a path of destruction?

Dreams—my dreams—were what my heart was aching for that day as I waited for the Lord to make our pathway clear. The last thing in the world I wanted was to stay right where I was, in this small town in Wisconsin, where winters could be so harsh.

Finally, the day arrived when our future plans became crystal clear. The corporation my husband was working for heard a rumor that he was checking out job possibilities with other companies. In fact, he had almost negotiated a deal with a smaller company when his current employer offered him a management position in St. Louis, Missouri. Included in the offer was a substantial pay increase and a new company car. They sent him to St. Louis and wined and dined him.

Knowing my husband the way I do, I knew the VIP treatment would not have any influence on his decision, but knowing the desires in the heart of the woman he loved definitely could. My husband believed we should be content in all circumstances. I know he would have been happy to live the rest of his life right where we were. He could also be equally happy living in a big city in Missouri.

The decision had been made to move and we sold our house. We packed our belongings and off to a suburb of St. Louis we headed. Driving across the Mississippi River to our new homeland was a sight to behold. The dazzling St. Louis Gateway Arch surrounded by the awesome skyline of the big city made my heart throb. My dream had come true; we were here. As we made our way through the bumper-to-bumper traffic, from one side of the city to the other, the excitement of this new venture overflowed within me. The days and weeks ahead would be filled with building a relationship to the wonder of it all.

Little did I know that glorious day would be the beginning of my lonely desert experience and I would never be the same again.

GOD BROKE ME

As we began to unpack and slowly, but surely turn our new house into our home, I felt something was missing. I wondered what it was;

after all, I had everything I ever dreamed of. All of my life I had been active in various things at church, school and in our community. This allowed me to feel complete. I was excited to see what I would be doing here, but the door to any ministry seemed tightly shut. I began to feel the presence of a cold steel wall separating me from the city I loved and the people who were a part of it. What was happening? The loneliness in my heart seemed to be more than I could bear.

In the past I have heard people say that God broke them. I never understood just what that meant, but God had begun the breaking process in my life. I did not even realize it. All I knew was that I did not like what was happening in my life because it was crushing my spirit. My heart ached. I felt like I was trapped in a *learning room.* I was continually learning about speaking and listening to God. I would spend hours desperately crying out to God, "What are you doing?"

Living in the Philippines, through all the difficulties, I began to learn what it meant to listen to that still, small voice within and not the voice of me. More often though, I liked what the voice of me was saying better. I would listen to that, not realizing who I was listening to. I have always been a strong-willed person, so for God to break that will took a lot of agony. The time had come for me to put all I had learned into practice in my own life.

In the beginning process of breaking, I would not always obey as God would speak, "Be still and listen." Without realizing what I was doing I would make my own plans. I thought I knew what needed to be done to fill the void in my life, but little did I know, God was going to use my rebellious spirit to teach me when I would listen to that still, small voice and when I would listen to the voice of me.

To add to the misery of what I was going through emotionally, we soon began to realize that living in a big city was much more expensive: food, car insurance, living expenses—everything. Plus, having an in-ground pool was very much a luxury expense. The weather was so much warmer that we used our air conditioner all the time—that is, until we got the first bill. Even though my husband earned a great salary we never felt so broke in our entire lives; even living on missionary salary in the Philippines was better.

I longed to fix up my new house just the way I wanted, but the money simply was not there. We had learned the hard way that charging was not the answer, so what were our options? I could find a job, but then I would not be able to volunteer at the kids' school or be there when they got home. I questioned, "Can I just trust God to provide for our finances? Do I need to learn to be more practical? Should I give up the desire for more things in my life?" I know in today's world, staying home is not always a woman's desire, but it truly was mine. I wanted to be there for our four sons. I felt committed to that, until things became financially harder. Then I started to rationalize that the kids were older now and if I got the right job, it could work.

The key word in this thinking was "I." Was I letting God lead me or was I leading the way? I believe at this time in my life God was saying "no" to me getting a job because He had other plans for me. He wanted to take everything out of my life so that I would "be still and listen." I did not like that idea. After all, I am a people-person who enjoyed being out there doing something to better my world, but when God wants to strip you bare you might as well give Him the control, because ultimately it will happen anyway. I would continually hear that still, small voice say "listen," and sometimes I would, but more often I would not and the pain would follow.

I had been waiting on God to speak to me about a job in my life, but I felt I could not wait any longer. I needed something in my life now. So, I would see a job in the paper that sounded good and I would call, set up an appointment and then live with the lack of peace. I was again seeking my own desires.

One of the first jobs I applied for was at a bank about three miles from our house. They called me for an interview and I excitedly pondered just what I should say and wear to make a good impression, but when the day of my interview arrived, I felt hesitation, as that still, small voice inside said,

"You should not be doing this!" The interview went well, but as I returned home the lack of peace within my heart over the job was overwhelming me. I began to question, "Should I have listened?" My desire was to have this job and I actually felt I needed it, but I had also learned through trials that if it is not what God wants for me, the joy would be lacking.

My heart ached as I realized I would have to call and turn down something I thought I wanted more than anything. When I picked up the phone to turn down the job offer, I did not have the strength to do it on my own. I said, "Lord, You must take control." He did. The perfect words to politely decline their offer came out of my mouth, almost through no effort of my own. God is so faithful, even though we are not. I had not listened to that still, small voice within. My desires had controlled me. When I realized I wanted to be obedient to God's desires, He lovingly took control and made it easier for me.

Immediately after I hung up the phone, peace overflowed within my soul. I knew I had finally been obedient, and even though the hurt of a missed opportunity was still present, the joy was overshadowing the pain.

One important thing that my first interview experience clarified for me was that I did not want a job that would take me away from my kids when they were on vacation from school. I applied for a job within the school system. There was one problem though; getting a job in the school system was next to impossible, especially with my lack of experience. The only experience I had was volunteer work in the kids' libraries, but with God nothing is impossible.

The only job I had heard about in the school district was a need for cafeteria workers, but that kind of work did not appeal to me one bit. My whole life had been cooking and cleaning, so why would I want to do this for a job? However, that little voice inside just kept saying, "Try it."

After resisting for a long time, I eventually submitted and applied for a job in the school cafeteria as a substitute worker. I was called to come in quite often. Every time I would put on my school uniform and go to work, God would chip away a little more of my pride. At first I would come home with red hands from the water and cry, "Why Lord?" Even though I was struggling with working at this job, I had complete peace knowing I was right where I was supposed to be. As time passed, I even began to enjoy going to work. The cafeteria workers were some of the most special, dedicated people I had ever met. It is extremely hard work, but each of them started out with the same reason I did—so they could be home when their kids were.

After working there a little over six months a miracle happened. I was on my way out the door when the phone rang. A woman from the school district was calling to tell me about a temporary part-time job in the library entering book information into the computer. Even better, the hours were flexible and I could choose what days I wanted to work. "Could you come in tomorrow for an interview?" she asked. Of course, I replied with a hearty, "YES!" I hung up the phone and knew without a doubt this was the job for me.

When I arrived for the interview, the principal said, "You came highly recommended." This puzzled me, as I did not know of anyone who would have recommended me for the job. I ended up getting the job and I truly believe that this was God's way of blessing me for being willing to give up my desires and go with His. My supervisor later told me that the women in the cafeteria told them they should hire me. She said, "Those ladies are hard to please and if they recommended you, you must be a good worker." A job I reluctantly took on turned out to lead me to truly wonderful things.

GOD BUILDS OUR FAITH

When we come upon the lonely desert times in our lives, we might think we are truly alone, but God is right there with us. We might not feel His presence, possibly due to sin in our lives, but He is there. He provides means to keep us going to give us the encouragement to continue on. He builds our faith. He is always there working on all things together for our good.

Yes, God was faithful to me during my lonely desert time. He did not give up on me, rather, He waited patiently for me to understand and obey. During that time, He provided someone to be there for me, to pick me up when I would fall, to encourage me and to love me. I had been married to this man for eighteen years, but God gave us a special closeness out there in the desert in which I will never forget.

You see, while many things were happening in my life, there was a tremendous task lying before my husband in his job. He did not realize it, but my husband was charged with turning this new office—the worst in the company—into an office like the one he left, which was the best in the company. My husband does not give up easily, so each day brought long hours as he tried desperately to turn the office around. It was a mess. The former manager had left many things in a mess. Dave had to organize it all. The employees did not work well together. The unions were hard to control. He worked feverishly everyday, but would come home feeling like he had not accomplished anything.

I had to take more responsibility of the kids because he would come home every night and fall asleep soon after supper. The pressures of changing things slowly began to take its toll on him, and on me.

My husband and I have always had a special relationship. We realized how important it is to spend time alone in a marriage, to just talk and share. We would go out one night a week for dinner. Every Saturday morning, before the kids would even wake up, we would go out and have breakfast and share the burdens on our hearts, oftentimes with tears. Those times together helped draw us closer, because deep inside we were both struggling.

I especially did not like what was happening to me as a wife. I saw myself becoming a "nagging wife." Whether I liked it or not, being a wife and mother gave me an enormous influence on my family. That influence could be Godly or it could be my selfish desires or thinking. I had learned many years ago that a "nagging wife" was not a good thing to be, but I was learning that there are different ways a woman can be a "nagging wife." She can be mean, bossy and say things over and over in anger. I might have been that type of nag when we first got married, but God had changed that in me.

Have you ever wondered if a woman can be a Godly nag? Well, that is what you could have called me. I was a woman who would spend a lot of time praying. Unfortunately, because of that, I unknowingly thought I knew what was best for our family, even more than our family's leader, my husband. If I thought I had a good idea about something, I would express it to my husband in a loving way. Rather than leave it at that, I would express it again and again in different ways until my husband would get tired of my nagging and give in. I am sure if anyone else would have acted like this toward my husband, he would have told them to quit bugging him, but he loves me and he wants me to be happy. After all, in a marriage relationship both parties should want to make each other happy.

To give you an example of my nagging, every Saturday night I would scour the ads in the paper for good sales, knowing we could not afford new things anyway. In this way I would put myself in the temptation to buy a good deal. (I have since learned not to even look at the ads unless I have something I need to buy.) I had a burning desire to buy a living room couch. The little voice inside was telling me we could not afford it, but my desire made me check it out anyway.

One day I saw a great sale on furniture. I mentioned it to my husband because we had no furniture in our living room. He said nothing. I wanted him to at least respond, but he did not, so I told myself I would not say another word. The day went on, and I just could not leave it alone. I hinted, "Boy, this ad says you have a year to pay for any furniture you buy. Can we go and at least look at it?" With a defeated look on his face Dave agreed.

I knew that "just looking" would not happen. We would get in that store and my lust for material things would take over and we would fall into the trap of putting something on credit. Sure enough, it happened. We rationalized that using our tax return money to pay for it was the answer. It would be several weeks before they would deliver our new living room furniture. During those weeks God began to work again on my heart and the peace of this purchase was missing.

Finally, I realized what I had done. I had manipulated my husband into buying that furniture and that was wrong. Now it was time to undo the mess I had made. It was not easy because my husband is the type of person who sticks to a decision once he has made it. I humbly told him I was sorry for what I had done and pleaded that he would let me make it right. He finally agreed and I cancelled the furniture and when we got our taxes back, we needed the money just to live on. If I had only listened to that still, small voice inside I could have saved us a lot of grief.

GOD KNOWS WHAT IS BEST

I learned many important lessons through these trials. Sometimes circumstances in our lives can convince us that God has answered our prayers. (Like the ad in the newspaper about the furniture on sale.) I believe that satan can use things like this to confuse us and draw us away from God's plan. This has happened to me more than I would want to tell.

I also learned that God truly does know what is best for me. He will show me if I will only listen. I think I know what is best, but through one experience after another God showed me that I really needed to listen to that still, small voice, even if it was not what I wanted. I realized that I needed to be willing to give up my desires and go with what He wants. There was one problem: How did I know which voice to listen to? I needed to know what God wanted before I could be obedient and listen. That is where the challenges came in.

THREE VOICES SPEAK

Three voices are continually speaking in our lives: our own voice, God, and satan. Often, I could not tell which voice was which. I was realizing through trial and error that the voice I was listening to the most was the loudest voice, which seems logical, but not when the loud voice is the voice of ME.

Soon, I began to realize how I made decisions. If a situation arose that required a choice, I would think it through and look at every possible choice I could make. It seemed there would always be one choice that I really did not like, but I would have to at least be willing to make that choice if that still, small voice would keep speaking in that direction. No matter how I felt about a particular situation, God would prove over and over how He knows what is best and I needed to trust Him. The fact is that with every mistake I would make, I learned a little more about how to listen.

VICTORY IN LISTENING

Through the trials of trying to listen to that still, small voice, there is not just defeat—there are victories too. One victory that I had involved the Cub Scouts. My son Aaron, who was eight years old at the time, wanted to be involved in Cub Scouts. During the first meeting they said, "We need a lot of help from parents or else Cub Scouts could not be a reality." I thought, maybe this is where I can become involved.

In the past I had received joy from doing Christian work such as Bible studies, women's groups, and Sunday school, but now I realized I needed to be out there in the real world, working more to be the missionary God intended us all to be. Cub Scouts sounded like the perfect way to do this.

My options for involvement were Cub Master, Committee Chairman, and Den Leader. Being a Den Leader for eight little eight-year-old boys did not sound like my cup of tea, but through all I had learned, I realized I would not close the door to this possibility. I had to be willing to choose this if God would lead me to do it.

Time passed and I was asked to be the Cub Master, which was the leader of the whole Cub Scout den. I felt the urge to become a leader again, but I could hear that still, small voice saying "NO." After I had prayed about it a lot, I knew this was not where I should be. I believed in my heart a little boys' group should be led by a man.

I feel sometimes that when women take control, men are let off the hook. I was beginning to wonder, "Is that why more men do not take over the leadership in their homes because we woman are too quick to do it?" Maybe men would get more involved in things if women would sit back and let them do it, even if it might take them longer to commit to something. I wanted to try this thinking in my own life. Being a leader, it is easy to take over. I wanted to try and let the men I come in contact with be challenged to be the leaders God would want. I told the group my reason for turning down the job of Cub Master, and soon after a man in the group volunteered. Praise God!

I felt that still, small voice saying that I should be a Den Leader. This thought did not excite me at all, but I knew from the pain in the past that seeking my desires and not God's plan for me brings more pain than it is worth. I prayed "God, I am willing to be a Den Leader if this is what you want." In the meantime, I met a woman who was also willing to work as Committee Chairman, but she said to me, "I do not want to do it alone. Could we co-chair this position together?" I told her "I will pray about it." I pleaded before God, "Please show me where you want me. I am willing to do whatever your will is for me." He answered that prayer in a way that I had no control over. The woman who had asked me to co-chair the position of Committee Chairman began to cause a lot of problems in the group. She eventually left after causing many problems for the den.

Yes, I ended up being a Den Leader. In the months to come I cannot tell you how many times I praised and thanked God for working it all out this way. I was so thankful that I had been willing to go with the task I really did not want because it proved to be the best for me. I praised God for leading me to become a Den Leader. I must admit even though the thought of being a Den Leader did not sound that great to me, I ended up enjoying it immensely.

I was beginning to realize more than ever that the God we serve is so faithful. When I would submit to the direction I believed God was leading me, even if I did not want to go in that direction, He would always allow me to enjoy that task and see why it was best for me.

I really do not know what is best for me, but God does, and the more I learn to listen to that still, small voice, no matter what it might be saying, the more joy I find in my life. If I listen first to that voice and then obey, I believe I can prevent heartache from falling into my life.

Above: This was our Church-house. You are looking at the back. The two windows upstairs and door on the left side of the picture is where we lived. The church would be the rest of the upstairs. A National Pastor and his family lived below us and another Missionary family lived below the church.

Below: Our family in a Jeepney.

It was a wonderful day when my mom and step-dad, Lloyd & Adeline Nyberg came to visit us. You can never imagine how wonderful it was to be with family again. They encouraged us more than they will ever know.

Howard and Carol Willson came and visited us for the weekend. It was wonderful to see friends from back home. We do not know how they stayed awake with the jet lag, but they did.

"Cinderella Pumpkin Van"
Above: Bill and Carol Wagner are a wonderful couple who allowed us to use their van for our summer of deputation and even a few months longer.
We will never forget their sacrifice.

Chapter 10

LEARNING TO OBEY

But if anyone obeys His word,
God's love is truly made complete in Him.
1 John 2:5a

The key to understanding is to truly take the time to listen to that still, small voice in our hearts and to the voice of God through His written word. Then when He speaks, we must obey. That is the hard part, and I was soon to realize just *how hard.*

I was living my dream—a loving husband, wonderful children, a dream place to live—but where was the joy? I was trying desperately to find it. Days, weeks, months, would pass but the haunting in my heart would not disappear. Is this truly what God wanted for our lives? Were we in God's will or were we in our will or, even worse, my will? Had my discontentment with small-town living created an influence in the life of my husband to the point that he was willing to make a decision to leave if that would make me happy?

This thought scared me. I reflected back to what had happened at the time of our decision to move here. I remembered how heavy my heart felt at the thought of spending the rest of my life in the small town where I grew up. It was terribly depressing for me. I really did not want to influence my husband's decision over what job to take, but he knew what the tears where saying.

We left the place that I did not want to call home and settled in the place of all my dreams and I was miserable. I kept reminiscing about the past and all I had learned about listening to the voice of God. Would I be willing to go with the idea I found least appealing? I was learning that what I wanted least could end up being what was the best for me. Could this be what had happened? Did God give me what I wanted most, yet it was not what was best for me? Did I need to realize this principle in my life?

LIVING SACRIFICE

As I continued to reflect, I believed that this is truly what God wanted to teach me. Romans 12:1 Paul says, "Therefore, I urge you brothers in view of God's mercy, to offer your bodies as living sacrifices, holy and pleasing to God--this is your spiritual act of worship."

I had prayed in the Philippines that I wanted to be a living sacrifice for God. I had no idea of what this really meant or how God would teach me about it. I did not understand how hard the learning process would be, but there was no turning back now.

What did I think it meant to be a "Living Sacrifice?" I believed that I should be willing to do whatever God wanted me to do, but I had to admit that this was not true. I wanted to do what I wanted much more. I heard the song "Living Sacrifice," and the words touched my heart. One of the lines says "Break down my will, make my desires your own." This is what was happening in my life. God was breaking my will and working to turn His desires into my own.

How was I going to put the principle of "Living Sacrifice" into practice in my own life? I had been so wrapped up in my dreams that I did not see that I was running away from God's voice. When I did not listen to that still, small voice, I would sin. I needed to take care of that. Next, I needed to give God the controls and be willing to go with His desires whatever they might be, realizing that is where true happiness is found.

This might mean that I might end up back in that small town, but I was now willing to go. Being in my own dreams, if it is not God's plan, brings only turmoil. Lastly, because I was here, there was nothing I could do but trust that God could work in His timing, for His desire, to be a presence in my life. There was only one thing I could do and that was to PRAY and then be willing to TRUST and OBEY.

I began praying, "God, if it is truly your will for us to move again, you need to work in the heart of my husband, because when he makes a decision, he sticks to it." I became bold in my praying. I knew my husband's pride might keep him from going back to the company he had almost made a deal with before we moved, so I prayed, "If this is where you want us, have the company call and offer Dave a job." I was not sure I should be asking God for such a definite sign, but I truly felt I needed that to keep my faith strong.

The months passed and my husband became more miserable in his job. I had never seen his spirit so broken about something. He was feeling defeated because the task was so awesome. Each day he would go to work, come home, and say, "I worked all day and I am no further ahead because of all the new business that has come about." My heart ached, thinking that we might be going through this misery, largely due to me and what I needed to learn. Of course God is so faithful, He can turn something terrible into something right.

WHAT IS GOD DOING?

God was chastening me in ways I had never experienced. The joy in my life was superficial. The learning was at times more than I thought I could handle. He was teaching me ways that I needed to change. The process of changing always brings pain, but God is faithful, even though I was not. He carried me when the pressures were unbearable and would send encouragement to keep me going.

A verse that became my strength was from Isaiah 41:10: "So do not fear, for I am with you, do not be dismayed, for I am your God.

I will strengthen you and help you. I will uphold you with my righteous right hand." I claimed this verse in my life because I simply could not continue on my own anymore.

Each day would bring more learning and more pain as I realized I could say that I wanted God's will, but my actions did not always show it. I would cry out to God, "*I cannot learn anymore.*" God knew just how much I could handle. He began to gently nudge me in a direction I did not want to pursue. My childhood hurts began to creep into my life. My father had been an alcoholic and when my life was hard I would eat to feel better. I started to see that I was doing the same thing now, but I lacked the energy to deal with it. That voice was prodding me, and for a few months, I would try and work through them by going to Adult Children of Alcoholic meetings. Eventually I felt that these issues were long past and I did not need any more hurt in my life. I became stubborn in this area and would not follow God's leading, but He would not quit nudging. He was working in my heart to soften it.

Time seemed to pass so slowly, but we had already been living in St. Charles, Missouri for a year. The discontentment in my husband's heart concerning his job was growing. His light was burning dimmer as each day would pass. His employer could see the discouragement in his eyes and tried to perk him by giving him incentives to stay, but the desire to achieve was dying. I knew that I was going to keep silent and let God work concerning my husband's future, but I felt there was one truth I must express to him. As I planned how I could share my heart with the man I loved, I knew the timing had to be at one of our evenings out.

We were sitting at one of our favorite restaurants, a quaint little outside cafe, on the cobblestone main street in our town. The late afternoon sun was beginning its descent toward the horizon. The cool breeze was refreshing our spirits. My heart began to race as we sat gazing at each other. How lucky I was to have this man just for me. I looked admiringly at his thick, sandy brown hair that ruffled with the breeze, his slight side burns, and those big blue eyes. His sexy smile warmed me all over. The love between us was more than I would have ever thought possible.

After moments of silence, each of us pondering the cares of the day, I began to share what was on my heart. "Dave, if you ever feel you do not want to take the stress of your job anymore, I want to let you know I am willing to move back to Wisconsin if that is your desire." Then I changed the subject.

I prayed daily, "If this is your will God, that we should move, please work it all out. It is in your hands." I must admit there were many times I did not want to wait anymore. I wanted to get out of there, but God was not finished with me yet.

CONFRONTING A CRUTCH IN MY LIFE

During the trials I was experiencing, I realized I was using a crutch to give me the joy I was missing. The thoughts that I was using food to help me to feel good surfaced again. The problem was that it would feel good at the moment, but suffering would follow because the foods I ate did not agree with my body. Once again I was hurting my body, my temple of God. I had conquered this problem while in the Philippines, but it was slowly creeping back into my life again. The discontentment of what I was going through made me reach out for sweets and soda instead of God. I would start by eating something sweet or drinking a soda and then binge until my body just could not take it any longer. I would become addicted to the caffeine and if I did not have it I became unbearable. I lived to eat and although I was not overweight, sweets and soda seemed to be the only things that would bring me joy.

This scared me because my father had been an alcoholic and I seemed to possess the same characteristics—except I did not drink alcohol. I believe this was God's way of nudging me to deal with my past. Each lonely day would pass and my true friends—my soda and sweets—would be there to cheer me up. I saw that I was getting out of control. I needed to get some help, but where? I scraped up enough courage one evening to go to an AL-ANON meeting, but I did not relate to their problems. I went to an Alcoholics Anonymous meeting and found I could relate to them more. Still, I did not seem to fit in.

I pleaded with God for help. I would try desperately to listen to that still, small voice regarding my eating habits, but my physical self would not listen. A verse in the Bible that God used to convince me was the same one that spoke to me in the Philippines, I Corinthians 3:16-17: "Do not you know that you yourselves are God's temple and that God's spirit lives in you? If anyone destroys God's temple, God will destroy him, for God's temple is sacred and you are that temple."

I was destroying my temple. I felt I was drowning in my sin. In a world where food is served wherever you go, the challenge of eating only truly nutritious food is a battle. I would eat healthly all week, and then I would fall apart on the weekends. I did hear God's voice directing me, but I wanted what I felt I needed. I was not truly willing to give up my desires, even though they were hurting my physical body in which God's spirit 1ives. How could God allow this to be happening in my life? With everything else in my life, how could He expect me to try and work this one out? As time passed, the answer became clear.

GOD'S PERFECT TIMING

Meanwhile, one night the phone rang. I picked up the phone and recognized the voice on the other end. It was for my husband. An hour later the conversation ended and Dave walked cheerfully into the room. He spoke the words I longed to hear. "That was my former company in Wisconsin. They offered me a job." The decision was made; we would be heading back to that little town in Wisconsin.

We still faced the challenge of selling our home. The economy in St. Louis, at this time, was bad due to several layoffs at large firms. Our suburb in particular was hit pretty hard. One day someone showed up unexpectedly at our front door and asked, "Could we look at your house?" Luckily we had cleaned the house just that very day in anticipation of an appointment that ended up being cancelled. The next day we had an unbelievable offer that we accepted on our house, but they had a house to sell. Their house sold in just six days. The timing was perfect for us to move just a week after our oldest son graduated from high school.

Why do we question what God is doing? His ways are not our own. His timing is absolutely perfect. He knows just how much we can take in any situation. He is there to guide us when the timing is right. As we again packed up our belongings to move on, I knew this was truly God's will. I had reservations about leaving this city of my dreams, but I knew it was time to go.

The memories of that place have never left me. It had been truly a lonely desert experience. I thanked God for the desert, for all He had taught me and for the ways He worked to change me. I praised God for being so faithful to me when I did not deserve it. I felt that for the first time I could relate to Jonah. He did not want to go to Ninevah as God had planned, but God just kept working so he would be willing to go. I was heading to my Ninevah and as tears welled up in my eyes, there was peace in my heart knowing I was not going alone. God did have a plan for me back in that little town of Stoughton, Wisconsin.

Chapter 11

COMING HOME

So there is hope for your future declares the Lord
"Your children will return to their own land."
Jeremiah 31:17

As we relocated to our new city, we trusted God to set our plan and show us a place to make a home. Going on the advice of some friends, we rented an absolutely beautiful home situated on the gorgeous Yahara River. The house was for sale, but they were willing to let us rent it. The difference in the cost of living from a big city to a small allowed us to be able to afford it. The view from the back of the house was breathtaking. I had never felt so relaxed as I did that month. It was as though God had allowed us this resting place, which was like being on vacation. The boys would walk out the back door down to the pier. They would put corn on the fishing pole as bait and then throw it into the water. It would not be long and they would begin reeling the fish in over and over again. The river was shallow so they would walk from one side to the other, screeching with joy.

We were able to enjoy the Fourth of July celebration from our back yard as the glare from the fireworks would reflect on the glimmering night waters of the river. Oh, how wonderful it would be to stay in a lovely home like this. Was this another of God's tests? We had a choice to make: We could live here and if it would sell we would have to move out within 30 days, or do we take a sure thing and rent another house. We had heard about another house that was available to rent for one year. It was nice, but nothing like the house we were currently living in. It had everything we wanted in a house, but it was not in great shape. We walked from room to room looking it over and then something unexpected happened.

When we left St. Louis, I prayed for something that God was about to answer. During my days in the Philippines and in my desert experience, I had grown and learned so much. I prayed to God, "I know you do not allow things to happen in people's lives without a purpose, so if it is ever your will for me to write about my experiences then you would have to provide for me a computer and a place to write." Up until now, I had forgotten that prayer.

My heart leapt when we walked into the next room. The woman said to me, "I hope it is okay if we leave our computer for you to use while we are away." She showed us the basement, where there was a beautiful office completely secluded from the rest of the house. That prayer came back to me at that moment, along with fear. Could God really want me to write about my experiences? I am not a writer. I left the house that day completely in a daze.

When we returned home, I looked around at the beauty of where we were living. I longed to stay right where we were in this lovely house on the river because it was close to town. I really did not want to move five miles out into the country where there was nothing but a few houses. Was I willing to give up my desire if God' s plan was different? Yes, all of my learning and all my pain were not in vain. If it was God's will for us to live in the country house, I must submit and follow God's leading because that is where true happiness will be.

My husband agreed and we did move into the house in the country. Before we even moved out of the house on the river, it sold. Another test had proven that I must listen to that little voice inside and not the voice of me.

We had barely moved in when my mother was admitted into the

hospital. She was very depressed and could not understand why. God used this in both of our lives to make us realize that our past had been difficult. We were definitely affected by living with an alcoholic and we had the choice of working out our past or sweeping the pain under the rug. God had been speaking to my heart regarding this in St. Louis, but I just could not listen. God was going to force me to do something about it now. I would look at my mother and see the pain that had been buried over the years and realize that I must be hurting deep inside too. If there was something I needed to deal with, I would rather do it while I was still young enough to handle the pain.

God allowed me to come across a book called *Love Hunger*, which opened my eyes. The first time I read it, I could see how my childhood had affected me tremendously. I began to realize that as a child I must have been hungry for love that my father just could not fill because of his alcoholism. To fill that void, I must have used food to make me feel good. God had changed me in some ways regarding this, but I could also see many ways I still needed to change. With God's help, I really did want to work on them.

I realized that we are all made up of body, mind, and spirit. God wants us to allow Him to work in all three areas. In the Philippines, He seemed to concentrate on working on my spirit. Then in St. Louis, He continued working there, but added the body and taking care of our temples. Now He was adding the mind, the emotions in my life. I felt like God was leading me to work, with His help, in every aspect of my life—body, mind, and spirit. I could obey or I could choose to ignore everything. My deepest desire is to be all God wants me to be. If that means experiencing heartache to change, I would not look forward to the hurt, but I know I would not go through it alone.

I continued reading the book *Love* Hunger, but I could only handle reading a few chapters at a time. The words were touching something inside of me. I needed to read it slowly and think about what I had read.

Then one day while I was slowly reading this book, I was suddenly overcome with emotions. Tears erupted as I let the pain spill out. It was uncontrollable and I kept repeating the words, "I never had a father." I tried to understand what this all meant. After thinking about it, I realized that even though I had a father, he had not met all of my needs.

It was an exhausting day, but when the tears settled, I was left with a feeling of freedom that was unexplainable. It felt wonderful.

After I finished the book I made an appointment with a counselor to evaluate, if in fact, I needed to work through anything else. I had a desire to really clean house and get all of the dirt out. I committed to God to work on it and let Him lead me.

After three visits, my doctor said, "I believe your Christianity has helped you work through your past. I do not think you will need to see me anymore." I praised and thanked God that day as I walked out of that office *Finally Free*. It was a new freedom and it felt wonderful. It seemed like the sun was shining more brightly. The birds singing could be heard more clearly. Yes, my past pain was gone. I was *Free*!

As I was working through all this, I felt it was time to get busy and begin writing. I had the computer now, but where should I begin? I prayed, "God show me if writing is truly what you want me to do. I do not want this to be my desire creeping in." God answered my prayer through my husband.

We were again out for our Saturday breakfast together, and my wise husband said, "I think you should begin writing that book that you have been talking about for so many years. God has provided you with the equipment, now get busy and do it." He continued, "You know you can spend all your days just working around the house, cleaning, but I do not think any of us would really even notice if the house has been cleaned or not. You need to forget about that so much and just write. See if this is what you are supposed to do."

I felt like crying. I needed to hear all that he said to me. He was right. I should try writing and see what would happen. I must admit there were days that I would rather have gone into town shopping or visiting friends rather than sitting at my computer trying to write. I felt so unqualified to be doing it, but I knew I would have no peace until I finished it. Each day I plugged away a little more, as time was running out on our year lease and my ideal writing space.

Chapter 12

HEEDING THE CALL TO WRITE

Come near to me and I will come near to you.

James 4:8

"Get busy and finish that book!" were the words I clearly heard from that little voice within.

"How can I?" I asked. "I am tired, I am worn out," but the words continued to stir within me.

Meanwhile, God had blessed Dave with a wonderful job. Our finances had improved immensely. The time had come for us to find our own home. The people that we were renting from would be back from their overseas assignment.

We started looking for the house that would soon be our home. I would call about a house or a lot suitable for building and the reply was always the same: "It is sold!"

"What is going on, Lord? It is only three months before we have to move. Where shall we live?"

Why is it that we have to worry about things? God does have a plan for our lives. We need to wait for Him. Sometimes it is challenging. We had learned from all of our experiences that most of the time God waits to the very last minute to open a door. Through these circumstances we learned to trust Him just a little bit longer.

People would often ask me if we found a house yet. My reply always came quickly, "Not yet, but I know God has something out there for us." As we looked at houses I could clearly hear that little voice inside saying, "Not this one, wait upon me." Sometimes I would listen and not even call about a house. Other times I was not so patient. I would look at a house and then realize I should have listened.

I was learning again what it means to listen to that still, small voice inside and then heeding the advice of my husband. When I would ask my husband about a certain house and he would say, "It is too small," or "I do not like that neighborhood," I would listen and not try to convince him that I liked the house. I longed more than anything to let God lead, listen to my husband's words and most importantly be willing to put my desires into God's hands and let Him turn His desires into my own.

In the meantime, as we searched for God's plan for our living, that little voice inside continued to harp, "Finish that book!" I realized I had nothing to lose by getting busy and finishing the book. Once it was finished, I could breathe a sigh of relief. I began to write daily so that when we moved from this place it would be finished. After all, I would no longer have a computer. I wondered if God was waiting for me to finish the task set before me before He would open a new door in my life. This motivated me to get it all done except for editing. Before I knew it our plans began to unfold.

One day a man stopped by our house to take a census of the kids who would be riding the school bus the following year. We chatted for a long time. Then I asked him, "By the way, since you get around as you do this, have you heard of any houses for sale?" He did know of a house and he described where it was. I thought I should at least drive by the house to see if we would like the area.

The next day I slowly made my way to the street he had mentioned. I looked at every house but did not see any FOR SALE signs. One house attracted me right away. I thought, "Could this be the house?" I finally called the number I was given to inquire which house it was. The man on the other end gave me the address and told me the price (which was exactly the price we could afford). As I again drove down the street I searched for house numbers and I wondered, "Could it be the one I wanted?" Sure enough, it was the one house on the street that I adored.

We called him back and made an appointment to see this house. The next day as we rang the doorbell, my heart fluttered with wonder at just what this house might look like inside. As the door opened, I could not believe my eyes.

We walked into a plush sunken living room with an ivory white fireplace. Above a massive bookshelf were mirrors that made the room look elegant. As we made our way into the kitchen, it was painted heavenly blue—our favorite color—with wallpaper that enhanced the room. Outside of the kitchen was a dog lover's dream. A completely fenced-in, shaded yard. Then came the final test, did it have something I longed for in my home—a master bathroom with a bathtub? We lingered in each room, enjoying all that we saw. Then the master bedroom was in sight. My heart raced as I made my way into the room. I opened the bathroom door and what did I see but a shiny white bathtub. It was a sight to behold.

We made an offer, wondering if this would be enough for them. They accepted it. We would be able to move into our new home at just the perfect time.

God is so faithful. We can rush ahead of His plans and miss out on the blessing He has in store for us. Each circumstance that comes along that we have to wait upon Him, the Lord will teach us so we will be able to wait a little longer the next time.

Chapter 13

AND THE WALLS CAME TUMBLING DOWN

Do not judge, or you too will be judged.

Matthew 7:1

We settled into our new home. Our oldest son, David, was in college. Our second son Jeremy attended Stoughton High School, our third son Andy went to the Stoughton Middle School and our youngest son Aaron was in fourth grade at Kegonsa Grade School in Stoughton. The boys could all continue on in the same schools that they had been attending.

We moved in August and by September the kids were all settled in our home and had started school. It felt wonderful to be in our own home again.

I finally finished writing my book. I put it on the shelf and left it in God's hands. If He wanted me to do anything with it, He would have to show me.

Now what should I do? After praying about it, I realized that I was finally free to get a job. I decided that I would like to work in the Stoughton School District. I wanted to be home when the kids were off of school. I applied for a position and ended up working six years in the Stoughton School District. I worked two years in Special Education at Yahara School and then four years as an Educational Assistant at Fox Prairie School. I enjoyed working in the Stoughton School

District.

Those six years passed very quickly and before we knew it all of our sons had graduated from high school except our youngest son Aaron, who was a junior in High School.

I realized with my sons older now, it might be a great time to explore the possibilities of a change in my work situation. There was a burning desire in my heart to try something new. I was off work for the summer, so I thought it would be the perfect time to check out my options. I applied at a Temporary Agency thinking I would work for the summer.

I continually told God that I was willing to GO wherever He would lead me. Then one day the agency called me and asked if I would be willing to work a three-week position in a church. I thought that sounded wonderful. I would love being around the ministry again, so I asked, "What church is it?" When she told me I thought, I don't know anything about this denomination, but decided to give it a try.

The secretary who trained me had been working there for years. She was seventy-plus years old and beautiful with snowy white hair and curls around her face. She always dressed nicely in outfits with coordinated shoes and accessories. I liked her immediately and we got along well.

One day when my three-week assignment was almost over, the pastor said to me, "Robin, will you come into my office?" I knew what he was going to ask me, but my heart was not sure I wanted to hear it. In this short time I had learned a lot of things that were very different from my denomination. I asked myself, "Could this be where God wanted me to continue working?"

I walked into the pastor's office and he asked me to sit down. He said, "You have been doing a great job and I would like to offer you a full-time position as a church secretary. We would like to modernize the office and we believe that you could help us do this. We need you here!"

I thought, "God, why can't you just put me in my own denomination?" I questioned if this was a good time for this church to have a new secretary. The current pastor would retire in one year and a new pastor would be chosen. Wouldn't it be better for the new pastor to choose his secretary? The years of learning made me realize that I could not close the door at this moment. I told the pastor I would pray about it and he asked if I could let him know by the end of the weekend.

I left there wondering what God was doing. I prayed all the way home and when I got there I fell on my knees and prayed, "Show me God!" I agonized all weekend, "Why here, God?" I was not sure that I wanted to go. It was stepping out of my comfort zone. I prayed, "Please show me before this weekend is over if this is truly where you want me."

I went about the weekend doing many things, but in my heart I was questioning, "Is this where God was leading me?"

Finally, it was Sunday night and nothing had happened to show me if I should accept this position. I told myself I would stay where I was in the school district.

Suddenly my doorbell chimed. I looked out the window to see who was there, but I could not see anyone. I did not recognize the car in the driveway. I opened the door, and there stood the pastor. He greeted me with a big smile and the most beautiful bouquet of flowers. It was a dozen roses: three pink, three yellow, three peach, and three white roses. My heart melted when I looked at them. He handed them to me and said, "We need you at our church!" We sat down and talked and he expressed his desire for me to work at this church. Before he left I had finally submitted and accepted the position. Years later as I told this story I said, "I think he manipulated me, but it worked!"

What would it be like working in another denomination that I was not familiar with? I did not know anything about their beliefs, but

I learned long ago that you might as well not try and run from what God is leading you to do.

What did God have in mind for me here? The questions swirled in my mind, but I knew I had to go.

What was holding me back from wanting to take this position? As I thought about it I realized that I had a wall that had built up in my life. What is a wall? A wall is anything in our life where our beliefs are so strong that we are closed off to any other way of thinking. What causes those walls to come tumbling down? When our eyes become open to new thoughts that challenge our thinking, the walls begin to fall down and our way of thinking slowly changes. How does this all happen? Who breaks down the wall? What if we are not open to allow our walls to be broken?

As I thought more about this I realized that walls in our lives begin at a very early age. I grew up in a Christian home. We went to church every Sunday. Even when we moved, we would quickly find a church to attend. As I grew up and started my own family, of course, we went to the same denominational church. We even spent three years as missionaries with our same denomination.

Now God was saying, "GO" to a different denomination.

The day arrived—my first day in my new position. I did not realize at the time what God was going to teach me in this place. You see I had the attitude that God was sending me there for what I could do for them, never realizing that it would be what they in turn would do for me.

Realizing that I was going to be the secretary for a church that was not my denomination was scary. What did this denomination really believe?

As I walked into the office that first day, I wondered how I could meet the challenges that this job would require. This office had been run the same way for many years. They wanted me to work at changing many things like set up a new voice mail system, organize the Rolodex, create a new church directory, organize the files and set up an oversized calendar for the church. I was overwhelmed. Could I really do all that was asked of me?

Each day I would meet a new person. I realized quickly what a warm and caring church this was. These people did not seem any different than the people in my own denomination. The wall was beginning to be chipped away.

How would the walls "come tumbling down?" God of course does all the breaking, but He uses people to do the chipping. God would bring many people into my life to chip away at my wall.

In the meantime, I worked hard at updating this office. I did not feel qualified to be doing any of it, but God would give me what I needed just when I needed it.

One day I was working at my computer when a virus alert appeared on the screen. What should I do? I said a little prayer and suddenly I thought of a man from this church who knew a lot about computers and I called him. He fixed the problem and continued to be my resource person. In my mind he was an angel sent from God.

The Bible verse 1 Thessalonians 5:24 says, "The one who calls you, is faithful and He will do it." Over and over I had to rely on God to do it. It was my only recourse, but He always came through. When God calls us to do something, we are not alone. He will provide what we need, when we need it. I have learned that God likes to wait until the very last minute to provide. Maybe that is so we learn to trust Him. I was learning that God was the ONLY one who could help me accomplish all that was before me.

As time progressed, a wall began to form in the relationship between the former secretary and myself. In any working relationship when you have the former and the current employee working together, the challenges can be great. Occasionally, I would try to talk to her about what was happening, but we were both so busy doing so many things that we did not have time to work on this relationship. But that is what relationships take—time.

Here we go again. God has allowed me to be in another situation like the Philippines? He put me in another relationship that was souring, one that we would have to work at to mend.

Many times I would swallow my pride and say I am sorry even though it was not entirely my fault. Other times I would realize that because I was doing what the pastor asked me to do, I could be hurting her feelings. He was my boss, however, so I needed to obey. I realized that if I communicated more with her, we would have a better relationship.

God is faithful. Within time, our relationship began to grow and flourish. We even went out to dinner together. This is the end result of God working in two people's lives to create unity in a relationship.

Life is filled with people and we can often hurt their feelings because of the busyness of our lives. We are too busy to stop and communicate. We do not want to take the effort to make things right.

Can you imagine how God must feel about us? He wants us to communicate with Him, but we do not take the time. We hurt Him by the things we do and say, but we are too "busy" to understand or care about what we are doing.

GOD STARTS CHIPPING AWAY

A year passed, and it was time for the senior pastor to retire. The board was looking at prospects to take his place. The interviews of the prospective candidates were set. We would meet them all.

I was able to talk with them all, but one pastor in particular impressed me. As we talked he asked me, "What do you think you offer to your position?"

I was very honest with him. "I am a people person and I love the people! When someone comes into the office that needs something or needs encouragement, that brings joy to my day. I am not a computer expert, but I care about the people."

He replied, "That is more important to me than computer skills." We had a great conversation.

Weeks later, he accepted the position of senior pastor. What would he be like to work for? What was God's plan for this man and the ministry here? On his first day, he walked into my office to say hello. I looked up at this tall young man. His hair was sandy brown and he wore it in a tidy manner. He had a kiddish smile with a warm attitude. I thought, "I think I am going to like this man." He seemed to really care about people.

This was his first pastorate on his own and he was excited about it. He had many great plans and ideas. Would I be able to keep up the pace with my lack of computer skills? The desire in my heart was not to become a computer expert. The passion in my heart was for the people.

We would sit and talk about the differences in our denominations. Our relationship began to grow and I realized that this man was truly a man after God's own heart (chip, chip). I must admit that I did not think that this is what I would find here.

I am not really sure what I thought it might be like in another denomination, but this man of God let the love of Jesus shine through in his life. He really practiced what he preached (chip, chip). It made a great impression in my life. We would talk about the differences in our beliefs without judging but tried to understand what the other one believed. We realized that what is important is our relationship with Jesus. All denominations have some differences in their beliefs. Some differences are about baptism, communion, speaking in tongues, whether we should have women pastors, but the core of all Christian denominations is found in JOHN 3:16:

For God so loved the world that he gave His one and only son, that whoever believes in Him shall not perish but have eternal life.

God loved us so much that He sent His son Jesus to die on the cross for our sins. If we believe in Jesus and trust Him as our Savior, we will have eternal life.

We worked together for the same cause in our own denominations (chip, chip). Together, we spread the love of Jesus to our world (chip, chip).

Of course, God put in my path many other people at that church who acted as chippers in my life. These people loved Jesus with all their heart. They realized how important prayer is and they practiced it (chip, chip). We prayed together even though we were from totally different backgrounds. They humbled me and made me realize that for many years I had been judging people who did not believe exactly like I did....That is sin. I needed to get down on my knees before God and ask His forgiveness.

It took God years of working in me to finally allow my wall to break down. God did the breaking, but He used people in my life to do the chipping. I have realized that nobody can really know what is in a church until you get inside of it. I am so thankful that God had put me inside of this church. It changed my life.

Chapter 14

GOD CREATED ME

For you created my inmost being; you knit me together in my mother's womb. I praise you because I am fearfully and wonderfully made; your works are wonderful, I know that full well. My frame was not hidden from you when I was made in the secret place. When I was woven together in the depths of the earth, your eyes saw my unformed body. All the days ordained for me were written in your book before one of them came to be.

Psalm 139:13-16

God created me. He knit me together in my mother's womb. I am, who I am, because God created me this way.

I grew up in a family of four girls. We all looked different, acted different and each had our own unique talents. Even though we came from the same parents, we were all totally different people.

Up until this point in my life, I thought I understood what my talents were, but working at the church helped me to discover something new about myself.

The clerical work day-in and day-out began to wear on me. I started to wither on the vine. I loved the people part of my job, but the computer part . . . well, it was not me. I was in a situation where I was not gifted. Every day as my work piled high on my desk, I was dying inside. Every request made of me required learning something new in an area where I did not fit. People would say to me, "My computer is not working. Can you fix it?" (Who, me? I do not know anything about that!) It was my job to get it done, so I would whisper a little prayer, "God, help me!" Another request, "Could you make this twenty-two page church bulletin in legal form like a book instead of regular?" I sat there in utter amazement. (I do not even know where to begin!) I would whisper a BIG prayer, "God, I need help NOW!" He would always come through, but the stress involved in accomplishing each request was slowly taking its toll on me. After four years of doing this, I was worn out.

I pleaded with God to lead me somewhere that I could use the natural gifts that He had given me, but He kept saying WAIT.

I struggled everyday. I asked myself, "How much longer can I continue on in this position?" I was trying desperately to figure out what the problem was. Then it hit me.

I was so busy working that my time with God was slipping away. I was trying to do this job on my own strength. In the beginning I knew I could not do this job without God, but in the end that is all I was doing. I was not spending time with God. I would ask him whenever I was in a pinch to help me out, but it was a one-sided conversation that was affecting me tremendously.

What was missing in my life? It was the same thing that happened to me in the Philippines and other times since. My time with God was missing. What happens then? I change! My attitudes and actions change and I lose the ability to hear the voice of God.

I remember back in the Philippines how my time with God disappeared and how it affected me. I thought I had learned my lessons, but here I was again in the same situation. Keeping God a priority in our lives is a lifetime challenge.

I realized that I needed to get up early before work and spend time with God—the one person who could help me to accomplish all that I needed to that day. Slowly my attitudes began to change. Making God a priority WILL change anyone! Just like relationships with people—we become like the people that we spend the most time with. We become more like God the more time we spend with Him.

Chapter 15

THE LEARNING CONTINUES

What He opens no one can shut,
and what He shuts no one can open.
Revelation 3:7b

After several months of submitting to God and spending time with Him, I began to think of possible job opportunities where I could use my people skills. That got me thinking about my mother, who was very interested in a ministry called Stonecroft Ministries. Their ministry involved a Christian Women's Club—a luncheon where women would come together to enjoy a nice lunch and hear a speaker who would share the story of how she came to know Jesus. Many people come to know Jesus at these luncheons.

My mother had been the founder of a vibrant and exciting CWC where she lived. She would share her story at the luncheons. I remember going around with her as she spoke. I felt so proud as she would share the story of our life in a loving way. The challenges of having an alcoholic husband and father piqued the interest of the women. Many families are affected by this addiction in some way.

As I looked back on my life, I remember a question I would always ask my mother: "How can you take so much and yet be so loving?" Her reply was always the same: "It is only because of the Lord; He gives me the strength." This made a big impact on my life.

God was the source of my mother's strength. She depended on Him moment by moment. Her words have left a legacy for my life.

As I reflected about my Mom's heart, I began to wonder if this would be something that I would enjoy. I checked out the Stonecroft Ministries Web site and saw that they needed National Representatives to travel around the country and start Christian Women's Clubs. A National spends six months in one area living in someone's home as she does this. As I inquired more about this, I realized they had never had a married National. I loved to travel and thought this would be a great way to use my gifts and abilities, but I had second thoughts about leaving my husband for that long. We talked it over together and decided that it was worth finding out more about it.

After filling out an extensive application, Dave and I were invited to Kansas City for an interview. Our time there began with a tour. It was so exciting to meet the staff of an organization that had been such a large part of my past. I would be proud to be a part of an organization that meant so much to my mother, a woman who truly put God first in her life. I wish that she could have seen me then, but I could only tell her the news; she was fighting Parkinson's disease and was not doing well.

After we had finished our tour and met the staff, it was time for our interview. They requested that Dave and I both be a part of the interview because they wanted his opinion also. As we talked with two of the women who ran the organization, I felt great admiration for them.

During the interview they asked us many questions about who we were. Dave was asked, "How would you feel about Robin being on the road so much?" His loving reply was, "It would not be my first choice to have her gone so much, but if this is what God is leading her to do, I would encourage Robin to do it."

We talked with them about many things that had happened in our lives. We felt that it was important to tell them that our greatest desire was to do whatever God would lead us to do. When we felt called to become missionaries in the Philippines, we obeyed. It was not easy. We packed up our four sons and said goodbye to our families and moved halfway across the world. Life was very challenging, but through it all we knew we were right in the center of where God wanted us to be. He was our strength, so if God were calling me to become a National with Stonecroft, He would be our strength. He would meet our needs and give me the abilities I needed to accomplish my task.

The interview went well, but the decision about my employment would take time. We all needed to pray about it. As we prepared to leave, we all got together and prayed for God's will to be done. Dave and I thanked them for allowing us to have this opportunity.

Before our flight home, I sat down for a few minutes to spend time reading my Bible and praying. I am not sure why, but I felt led to Revelations. I began reading here and there, waiting for the words of the Bible to speak to me. Then a verse popped out at me. Revelation 3:7b says, "What He opens no one can shut and what He shuts no one can open."

Was this going to be a door that would open that no one could shut or would this door close for me in this ministry? Only time would tell. We had to wait and let God move if this was meant for our lives.

A few weeks later, I was sitting in my office, feeling frustrated with the tasks in front of me. In the next few minutes, something happened that would change my life forever.

The phone rang. It was one of the women I had interviewed with at Stonecroft Ministries. "Good morning, Robin. I am happy to tell you that you have been accepted to be a National with Stonecroft Ministries!" I wanted to cry! Could this really be happening?

Minutes earlier I had been sitting at my desk questioning how much longer I would be here. I love the people, but the work is not where my gifts were. I earnestly prayed that God would give me a glimpse of my future.

I hung up the phone and wanted to dance around the room. God was finally opening a door where I was gifted. I could hardly contain myself. God was giving me the opportunity to share Jesus with people. I could hardly believe my good fortune. The decision was made and I was praising God. I still had a number of months to wait to be a part of the National Workshop, so this gave me some time to rest.

As the time drew closer, however, I found the peace was lacking in my heart. I asked God, "Are you leading me to decline this position that is my desire more than anything?" I must admit I felt confused and angry. Why would He answer my prayer when I asked, "Please God give me a glimpse of my future" with a call from Stonecroft?

My life seemed to be a series of tests. I would feel like God would say, "Go" and I would finally go and then He would say, "Turn directions now and GO another way." I had grown used to this happening. I was slowly learning not to fight it, but to obey. I knew I had to listen even though I did not understand its meaning.

It was with a heavy heart that I shared with the leadership of Stonecroft that God was closing the door on my opportunity to be a National. I did not understand at all the "whys" of this, but I knew I must obey.

"Where do you want me now God?" I pleaded! He confirmed completely that there was a plan of what He wanted me to do, but for now all I could do is WAIT until that plan unfolds.

Chapter 16

THE LISTENING ROOM

"Speak, Lord, for your servant is listening."
1 Samuel 3:9b

Years passed and the listening and learning continued day-in and day-out. One by one all our boys graduated from high school and it was just Dave and I. We had lived in the same house for eight years and we were getting tired of all the work involved in owning a home. Our house was about thirty years old now and many things needed to be replaced. Every weekend we wanted to do things that were fun, but it seemed like we were mowing the lawn, trimming bushes, or painting something. Dave and I sat down and talked about this. I asked, "Do you want to do the things involved with maintaining our home or should we sell it?" Dave responded, "Let's sell it."

We put an ad in the paper the next weekend. The market was pretty hot at this time and by Sunday we had two full priced offers. We were overwhelmed. It looked like we would be moving, but where?

I had a garage sale and almost as a joke I put up a sign that we had furniture to sell. A lady came and looked inside and bought all of our living room and bedroom furniture. I guess she liked the way it looked because she even bought the matching rugs from the floor. We wondered where we were going that all of our furniture sold.

We were in a whirlwind. Everything was happening so fast.

Before we knew what hit us, we moved into a nicely furnished temporary apartment. All along we continued to pray, "God, we will go wherever you lead us." We were beginning to understand what Abraham and Sarah must have felt. God said, "Go," and they packed up everything and went. This is what we were doing. We had been down this road many times in our lives and God was always faithful. We believed He would not stop now. In the perfect timing we would know.

We enjoyed this new resting place. It was in the middle of the city of Madison, Wisconsin, but you felt like you were in the country. It was peaceful and quiet. The complex was completely surrounded by trees. We had a pool just outside our door that was so refreshing. I would get up just as the sun was peeking through the trees and swim laps. We liked not having the responsibilities of a home.

After living in the temporary housing for over a year Dave suggested to me, "Why don't you go to Florida and visit your sister!" It had been a long winter. He knew I had been working hard on all of my writing and thought I might need some sister time. My sweet husband is so wonderful.

Before I knew it I was driving to Florida. I spent a lot of time praying along the way. I relaxed and did whatever I wanted. Having a family of five men—a husband and four sons—it is not always easy to do what *I* wanted.

The first night I stopped at a hotel. After I unpacked I began to plan for an early start the next morning. Then it hit me: Dave was not with me. He was the early riser, not me. I could get up whenever I wanted and leave, so that is just what I did. I slept in, took a refreshing swim in the indoor pool and ate a leisurely breakfast. Finally at about 11:00 I packed my car and headed through the mountains.

It was totally awesome sitting on the edge of a crystal clear lake surrounded by the mountains of the Cumberland Gap. The peaceful feeling that enveloped me can never be explained.

It took four days for me to get to Ft. Lauderdale. When I arrived, my sister set me up with the best sleeping arrangement. She wanted me to stay in her gorgeous pastel color bedroom with a mammoth king-size waterbed that overlooked the man-made lake in her back yard. It was relaxing and wonderful. My whole visit gave me time to spend thinking and LISTENING to God through the words of the Bible and that still, small voice inside.

Then the day arrived that I needed to head for home. I packed up my car and headed across Alligator Alley—the flat, straight highway next to a river that is home to all kinds of alligators. While driving across this long stretch of pavement, I finally submitted to that still, small voice from within. Tears began to well up in my eyes. I could not see the road so I pulled into a little rest area. I believed that little voice inside was telling me to let go of the book I had spent years writing. How could I do that? I had worked so hard on it and been through so much.

I prayed, "I do not understand why God. Who have I been LISTENING to, *me*?" That is what hurt me the most: the thought that I had been listening to *me* instead of God. Tears were streaming down my face when I finally said the words that tore my heart apart. I reached my hands to heaven and sobbed, "If that is what you want God, I will do it!" I could hardly contain myself.

After many minutes of sobbing, I got back in my car and cried across the whole state of Florida. What was I supposed to do with my life? Who was I LISTENING to? I had thought the whole time that I was supposed to write this book.

With exhaustion over my entire body, I finally arrived at my hotel. I could not cry anymore. As I made my way to my room, I glanced over my shoulder and saw a gorgeous pool. It was just what my aching body needed. The sun had already set. The stars were shining in the sky as I floated on my back across the water.

I did not even care to eat that night. I climbed into my bed not having any idea what my future would hold. "What would I do?" echoed over and over in my mind.

When I arrived home I was very discouraged and just did not know what to do. Dave and I needed to find a new place to live. The temporary housing was expensive and we had decided that when I got back from Florida, we would look for a different place.

I began to pray about our next step in our journey of life. Where would we live next?

After what had happened in Florida, I could not understand why, but I still believed that I was supposed to write. I prayed again, "God if you want me to write, provide us with a place that is so inspirational that I will know it is from you.

We looked around at many houses and could not find anything we liked so Dave suggested, "Maybe we should rent an apartment to see if we might like living in a condominium." That same day I drove past an apartment complex that looked inviting. It looked like a little city because it had everything you might need within walking distance. There were restaurants, a grocery store, a coffee shop, a health food store, a florist, an ice cream shop and even a place to get a manicure.

I thought it might be expensive, but I decided it would not hurt to look at it. I went in and met a woman named Julie. She was a sweet looking young woman, with shoulder length brown hair and a nice smile. I asked her if I could see an apartment in the new building. Now, there were only two buildings and neither one of them were old, but I liked the newer one. She said, "There's a real nice apartment in the older building." I tried to convince her to show me the one in the newer building, but for some reason she wanted to show me a different one.

I realized through all of my learning that I think I know what is best, but over and over God has shown me differently. He is the one who knows what is best, so I told Julie to show me the one she had suggested.

I could never explain completely what I felt when I walked into that apartment. It was magnificent. As I walked from one room to the next I knew this was the place for us. The view was breathtaking. It overlooked the bike trail that I rode on daily. Then we walked into the master bathroom and I was overwhelmed with joy. There was a sparkly white Jacuzzi bathtub, with two windows immediately above it. The sun was shining brightly throughout the room. The view outside of the window was heavenly. There were trees everywhere you looked. It was completely private and gorgeous.

I knew at that moment, that I was indeed supposed to write. This was the perfect writing place that I had asked for. I was puzzled as to what I was supposed to write, but I trusted that I would know.

After we moved into this writing sanctuary, I spent many months alone LISTENING and pleading with God to show me. "I questioned what I was supposed to write, if not my book?" I would spend hours every day trying to LISTEN to that still, small voice within. I tried writing many different things, but it did not give me any direction.

FINDING MY LISTENING ROOM

I began to think about my life and my times with God and I realized that I love spending time with Him. It would be the high point of my day. After examining what I did, I realized that I always found a place wherever we lived that I would go to spend time reading my Bible and praying. I would make it just the way I liked it, so I would want to go there. I called my place "My Listening Room."

Embracing this idea, and feeling fortunate to have found a perfect listening room in our new home, I started to spend some time looking up scripture and writing in my journal. Over the years I had always written a journal of my prayers to God. I began to write to God like I was talking to Him and filling in scripture when He would speak back to me. I loved doing this.

Daily I was in scripture and I began to remember something people would ask me over the years: "It seems like you like to study the Bible. What do you do?" Because of their curiosity, I began formatting my studies into various subject areas that people could follow. Thus, the Bible studies, He is SPEAKING! Are we LISTENING? were born.

I had gone to my sister's in Florida in January. On my way home I had felt led to let my book go. It was hard, but I did. Now I could see why. If I had not let the book go, the Bible studies might not have been born.

I became excited about my ideas and realized this was the writing I needed to do. I should write topical studies that were easy and simple for people who want to get into the Word, but did not know where to begin. When people would tell me about personal challenges, I would write titles for that subject and then begin writing and searching scripture for answers to life's issues. It was deeply rewarding and fulfilling for me.

One day God brought a great blessing to me. My son Andy's girlfriend said she would like to try out my Bible studies. She did not know that much about the Bible, but she wanted to learn more. This thrilled my heart that she would be willing to do this. After she finished, she told me, "I really like the confession part of the studies." I asked her why, and she replied, "It just made me feel so fresh inside!" My heart was so encouraged to hear her words.

Many other events fell into place to encourage me on this path. My son shared with me that his high school teachers always told him that he was a good writer. I had never known this. It opened a door for us to work together on the Bible studies, with Andy editing them for me and giving me lots of helpful advice. As we would sit together and talk about the studies, I could see great wisdom in my son. I felt so blessed to have his help and to know that he believed in me.

Another event encouraged me along my path. One day as we were editing the Bible studies, Andy suggested we create a website for the Bible studies. When I asked what it would cost, he worked it out on the Internet and said, "$41!"

"Let's pray about it." I said. "If we are supposed to do this God will provide."

Suddenly, I remembered a checking account that I had opened years earlier hoping to use for my ministry ideas. I said, "Andy, let me see how much I have in that account. I do not use it, but maybe there is some money in it!" I found the checkbook after some searching, and wouldn't you know it: the balance was exactly $41. We knew this was what we were supposed to do, so with Andy's great wisdom, he set up my very first website for the Bible studies.

Encouragement came in other unexpected ways. Once I had given one of my Bible studies to a friend, Bob Battermann, who had just lost his beautiful wife Lucile. It was called, "I Lost Someone I Love." I had not heard anything back from him. Then one day I was questioning all that I was doing, and I cried out to God, "I cannot take it anymore. If you want me to keep working on these studies, please show me or otherwise I want to quit."

A few minutes later the phone rang. It was Bob. He said, "I just wanted to tell you how much I liked your study. You put a lot of work in it." The minute I heard those words I was overwhelmed with emotion.

I told him, "I had just prayed that if I was supposed to continue writing these studies that God would show me otherwise I had to quit."

He said, "You cannot quit, these are great!"

Then there was another time I felt I just could not go on. Our finances were out of control. I needed to get a job, and I was ready to quit the Bible studies. I prayed for God to send some encouragement if

I was supposed to continue writing them. Just a few minutes later, my son David called. He said, "Listen to this!" He started playing some music with my daughter-in-law, Stacy, singing. I asked what it was for. He said, "It is for your Bible Studies!" As I listened to her sing, I cried and cried. God did not want me to quit. About six months earlier I had told David that one of my greatest desires for my studies would be to have Stacy sing the music in them. Music would make the studies more meaningful and nothing would make me happier than to have someone I care about do the singing. She had not replied back to me, so I thought that she did not want to.

This day made me realize that I needed to continue writing these studies. Years of learning, writing, and more learning continued. I had spent four years of my life writing full-time.

Over the years I realized that if I wanted to make God a priority in my life, I needed to STOP and make time for Him. Then I would go into my listening room and speak to Him with my prayers and then listen to Him from the words of the Bible.

My son Andrew setting up our first
He's SPEAKING! Are we LISTENING?
website.
www.hesspeakingarewelistening.com
Below
Andrew working on publishing this book.

Chapter 17

A VISION OR A PASSION

Again Jesus said, Peace be with you!
As the Father has sent me, I am sending you.
John 20:21

What is a vision? I had no idea, but I knew I was passionate about what I was doing. I was spending a lot of time learning about that still, small voice inside of me and realizing how much God wanted me to take the time to speak and listen to Him daily.

One day I was talking to the Pastor from the church I had worked at about a retreat we were working on. As we talked, he mentioned a good book for me to read called *Visioneering* by Andy Stanley. He said, "I will let you borrow my copy, but I will need it back in two days." I left his office with the book in my hand.

When I returned home I had so many things to do that I put the book on my nightstand and did not think much more about it. One day went by, then the second, and I never even started to read the book.

Then the night before I was supposed to return the book, something startled me from a deep sleep. Opening my eyes, I realized that the light on my desk was on. I slowly got up and went to shut it off. As I turned to get out of bed, I noticed the book on my nightstand. Since I did not have the chance to read it, I picked it up, went into the living room and sat down on my soft couch, wrapped a fluffy blanket around me and began reading.

The book spoke to my heart. I could not put it down. I spent the whole night reading the book until it was finished. I realized for the first time that I truly had a vision or passion that I believe God had planted in my heart. The following are several quotes from the book:

> Visions are born in the soul of a man or woman who is consumed with the tension between what is and what could be. Anyone who is emotionally involved, frustrated, brokenhearted, maybe even angry about the way things are in light of the way they believe things could be, is a candidate for a vision. Visions form in the hearts of those who are dissatisfied with the status quo. There is always a moral element to a vision. Vision carries with it a sense of conviction. (Page 17)
>
> Visioneering is the course one follows to make dreams a reality. Everybody ends up somewhere in life. A few people end up somewhere on purpose. Those are the ones with a vision.
>
> A clear vision, along with the courage to follow through, dramatically increases your chances of coming to the end of your life, looking back with a deep abiding satisfaction, and thinking, I did it. I succeeded. I finished well. My life counted.
>
> Too many times the routines of life begin to feel like shoveling dirt, but take those same routines, those same responsibilities and view them through the lens of vision and everything looks different. Vision brings your world into focus. Vision translates into purpose. A vision gives you a reason to get up in the morning.
>
> Until we discover His purpose and follow through, there will always be a hole in our soul. God has a vision for your life. What could possibly be more fulfilling than that? Missing out on God's plan for your lives must be the greatest tragedy this side of eternity."

When I finished reading this book I realized that I did have a vision. I had always thought of it as a passion, but whether it was a vision or a passion, it had motivated me in all that I had done.

There have been two passions throughout my life: Salvation: Bringing people to a saving knowledge of Jesus Christ. Growth: Helping them to stop their busy lives and find time for God.

While I had been writing the Bible studies, I was also thinking of ways to get them out. How could I help people to understand how important it is to STOP and go into their LISTENING Room to spend time with God, their Creator?

We as humans need to spend time with God. This is how we understand what we need to do in our lives. When challenges come along, He gives us what we need to handle them. If we are not spending time with Him how can He encourage us and give us the strength to do what we need to do in our lives.

Do you have a vision or a passion in your heart? You might ask, "What is a passion?" For me a passion is something that is constantly on my mind. I want to share it with everyone I can because I believe in it.

Over the years I have been curious about passions or visions in peoples' lives, so I would interview people about it.

One day I was working at the election polls. It was a very slow election day. I looked around the empty room. All of the poll workers were sitting there doing nothing so I decided to ask them, "Do you have a passion in your life?" One lady in particular was very interesting to me. When I asked her she said, "Oh, I have a lot of passions." She began to tell me about some of the things she liked. As I listened I would ask her different questions to see if I could pull a passion out of her. Suddenly she started talking about something in her life and she became excited in what she was saying. Her whole personality had changed as she told me all about it. I believe her passion had come to the surface.

God plants visions or passions in our lives. If you do not know if you have one, ask God to show you. He will. I do not know when or if I will ever have an opportunity to change the world with my passion, but I do know God is in control. When I spend time speaking and listening to him, He will guide me and direct me into the paths that are needed to fuel my passion into reality.

Chapter 18

GOD, I DO NOT UNDERSTAND

You are my lamp, O Lord; the Lord turns my darkness into light.
2 Samuel 22:29

I began diligently working on the Bible studies and the LISTENING Room ideas, but because I was not working, our funds were slowly disappearing. I asked God, "What should I do? I need to make some money!" I was confident that He would show me.

I woke up suddenly one night. As I lay there silently wondering why I was awake, the Bible verse "This is the way, walk in it!" entered my mind. My thoughts unexpectedly turned to two organizations that I had been involved with over the years. I had been praying that God would lead me where He wanted me to go. I questioned if this was His answer.

I was already involved in one of the organizations that had popped into my head. I had been working as a volunteer. I believed in what they were doing because they were helping women realize the importance of God in their lives. This involved my passion so it was a perfect place for me to volunteer.

Now the other organization, I had not been involved with them. They helped women feel beautiful on the outside with their facial products.

Many years ago, when I was a young woman, I started wearing

some of their facial products and loved them. In fact, it was now twenty-five years later and I still use these products, so I decided to call someone I knew who was a part of this organization.

We talked together and she shared with me how much she enjoyed working there and how it gave her the flexibility to still be a mother and do other things. Before the day ended I had signed up to be a sales person in this organization.

I believed if I were going to sell any women's products in my life, this would be the one I could sell because it had worked for me.

I could not understand why God was moving me in this direction, but I decided that I had to go there. I had never thought of sales as a position for me, but it would be a job that would offer flexibility to continue writing. I would be able to make some money doing this, but the question that tore my heart apart was, "What was happening to my passions and my dreams?" This direction in my life was definitely not part of MY plan.

Dave and I talked about this and he suggested that I take it slow. You would think after all of my years of learning, I would have heeded his advice. Instead, I plunged into this, thinking this would be a great way to make money to fund everything that I wanted to do.

The key word in all of this was "I". That little voice inside of me seemed to be saying "You are taking your finances into your own hands," but I was not listening because I wanted to finally earn some money.

I began my sales position believing that I would make enough money to fund my dreams. I went into it full force.

For three years I wore myself out trying to make the money I thought I needed to fund my plan, but it consumed me. I was frustrated all the time.

The interesting part about it was that I was really good in my sales position. I would walk down the street with a basket of products in it, and women would come up to me and buy something. I would pray that I would sell a certain amount in a week and it always happened, so what was the problem?

The problem was that I did the work to the extreme instead of heeding my husband's advice and doing it slowly. If I had done it slowly, I could have made a little money and still continued my writing. Instead I was running around like a crazy woman trying to make money. It got out of control.

The Bible tells us in 1 Timothy 6:10, For the love of money is a root of all kinds of evil. Some people eager for money have wandered from the faith and pierced themselves with many griefs.

Wow, what an eye opener. How had this happened to me? Money had never been my motivation for anything, UNTIL NOW. I had been working so hard trying to make money and in reality I was losing money.

God is so faithful. He did not give up on me. He waited quietly for me to discover what I was doing in my life.

Each day I lacked motivation. I could not work in my office any longer. The burning passion for writing and spending time in my listening room began to fade. What should I do? I was desperate for answers, so I did something very unusual. I took everything off of my desk. I put EVERYTHING in my office on one side of my room. Then I covered it all. I prayed, "God, I give it all to you and please just give back what you want me to do."

The first morning after I did this, I sat down at my computer and began writing a new Bible study. It all came together and it felt so good. Whenever I would question whether I should continue with the Bible Studies, I would always get the encouragement I needed to keep them going. Suddenly everything felt restful. I loved it.

Meanwhile, I returned to my LISTENING Room and confessed my sins to God. If I had run from His plan I was indeed sorry, but there was no turning back.

Confession always brings joy. My time in my LISTENING Room began to flourish. I was again motivated to get back into my writing again.

There are times in all of our lives where we run around doing our own thing. We think we are doing what God wants, but when our eyes are finally opened and we confess our sins to God, He can turn it all around and make something good out of our mistakes.

I believe with all of my heart that I was supposed to be involved in both of these organizations because being in them taught me many valuable lessons, but the time had come to let them go.

During this time in my life there was a movie that spoke very clearly to my heart. The main character was spending a lot of time running around doing what he thought he wanted but was miserable. After doing this for quite awhile he finally fell to his knees and cried out to God that he did not want to do what he wanted with his life, but he wanted to do what God wanted. Then at the end of the movie God spoke to the main character with some very powerful words. He said that people should not wait for a miracle to happen in their lives, they should instead be the miracle.

Chapter 19

A STRAIGHT PATH

Trust in the Lord with all your heart and lean not on your own understanding; In all your ways acknowledge Him and He will make your paths straight.

Proverbs 3:5-6

Even though I loved our apartment with my writing space and LISTENING Room, I longed to be settled in our own home. I wondered when we would have our own home again. Then a thought popped into my head: I had prayed that if I was supposed to write, that God would put me in a place where I could write. I was in that place now. Had I finished my writing? I answered emphatically "NO!" I had been so wrapped up in my sales position that I had totally let my writing go. When I thought about this I wondered if maybe the reason for the delay in our getting settled had to do with the fact that I had not finished the work that I was called to do.

I pulled out my diaries and my writing and began working on updating my book. I had lived a few more chapters that had to be written. As I looked over everything, I was so glad that I had done some writing that would make it easier to actually finish the book.

An upcoming writer's conference caught my eye. I had just told Dave if I could do anything I want, it would be to write and speak about all the things that God had been teaching me about listening to Him. I prayed that if I was supposed to go to this conference that the money would be provided. I decided I would ask the conference if they ever give discounts. The day I finally finished a big section of the book, I received an e-mail saying I could come to the conference for half price. That was my answer. God had provided just enough money for me to go.

I said to Dave, "Do you want to go to this conference with me? I would be paying for the room anyway and you could spend some time to yourself doing what you want."

He thought about it and then said, "Let's go!" So together we set out for Minneapolis, Minnesota.

The first day of the conference went well. I was glad I had gone and I learned a lot. I still kept questioning if I was a writer. I had a brief consultation with one of the writers and I told him how God had provided a computer for me when I first began writing and how God had led me. I proceeded to tell him, "I am not a writer." He looked at me intently and said, "Yes, you are. You are a writer!" I thought a lot about that, but still lacked confidence.

The second night that same writer put on a wonderful skit: An old man came to his home one day and took him outside to an elevator that went down, down, down. By his description, you knew that he was talking about hell. Then he met someone who said, "You, I know you and you are a writer."

He said, "No, no I am not."

The other man said, "You were going to write an article on evangelism. Oh, you never did." A similar thing happened several times and he always denied that he was a writer. Then he went back in the elevator, and he went up, up, up and you knew he was talking about heaven. A little girl came up to him and said, "I know you, you are a writer."

He answered, "Yes I am." Then she went on to say that the book he had written had the plan of salvation in it and after reading it she invited Jesus into her life. Several other people had similar stories.

Then he thought, "What if I had never written?"

It was a tearjerker. I was touched and moved. I thought, "I can keep denying that I am a writer, or I can just do it." Another session followed that skit, but my heart was too moved to concentrate. I needed to be alone. I went outside and saw the sliver of moon up in the star light sky. I looked up at it and said, "Yes, God! I will write if that is what you want me to do. In fact, that is what I would like to do."

When I got back to our room I asked Dave if he would pray with me. This was my prayer:

Dear God,

I would like to write. I feel like I have a lot to say, but you know our finances are a mess. I have been trying to make money to pay-off our debt, but it was not working. I feel like you keep saying, "Trust me." It is hard when the money is disappearing, but I know I need to trust you. God, if you want me to write please provide a home for us, that we can afford, that has a breathtaking view so I know that it is from you.

With that, I put everything in God's hands and waited for Him to show me the way.

I had barely finished updating my book when God graciously opened the door for us to finally find our own home again. It was not long and we moved into our very own condo on the bike trail where I always rode my bike. It was a hide-a-way in the center of the city of Madison. It was secluded in the middle of the woods. The view from the window above my desk was indescribable. As I looked out the window I felt enclosed in the woods, with the sun's rays beaming here and there. Little patches of blue sky could be seen in between the leaves of the trees. It was heavenly. God is so good. My heart was so encouraged with my dream writing place, my home in the woods.

Chapter 20

CLARITY AT LAST

For I know the plans I have for you, declares the Lord, plans to prosper you and not to harm you, plans to give you hope and a future.
Jeremiah 29:11

I left the writer's conference with a burning desire to write.

What a journey this has been. Sometimes I wondered if I would ever make it to the end, but I trusted that God would help me each step of the way. I have discovered in any situation we can look at the possible options in our lives. We could even make a list. As we look to where God might lead us, we MUST be willing to go to the place that we least desire. It might not mean that God will lead us there, but we need to be willing to go, if He did. Then if we see him leading us into the direction that we do not like, we must believe that once we submit and are willing to go, He will show us why it was best for us. It might only be for a short time that we will be there, but we can trust that He knows what is best. I have discovered more often than not, something will happen that you had never thought of. A totally different direction will arrive.

The challenges of sitting quietly and listening to the still, small voice in my heart, at times, made me want to give up all that I felt I was supposed to do. I would cry out to God, "I cannot take anymore!" and he would lovingly send something or someone along to encourage me. God is faithful. When He calls us to do something, we are not alone. We might feel like it at times, but we are not. I have discovered first-hand that if I go in a direction that I do not particularly want, but He leads me there, after a while I realize that He put me there to learn something.

Are you in a desert in your life? Are you looking for God to put you somewhere? The advice I would say to you, which I did not use myself, is do not keep waiting—bloom where you are planted.

Epilogue

The END, The BEGINNING

We (I) will LISTEN and OBEY.

Deuteronomy 5:27b

"Robin, you need a vacation" were the words my friend shared with me.

"I think you need a vacation," said another friend. Throughout the past seventeen years of learning, these women had been a sounding board for me. I shared with them many of the things I had gone through in learning to LISTEN to that still, small voice inside. They realized I was at the end. I could not go on walking by faith and not seeing the end. I was tired, weak and worn. Now I had gotten into this condition on my own accord. Listening to God does not tire you out, disobeying Him does.

When each of these women told me that I needed a vacation I was a little taken aback. What exactly did that mean? Did they think I was crazy? Maybe they realized because I was a dreamer, I was always thinking about something. Anyway, when they shared this with me, I was happy to tell them that Dave and I were already planning a vacation. My friends suggested that I take some time and rest until we left. Their advice helped me to realize how important it was for me to do this.

The day arrived for our vacation. It would begin in a wonderful way with all of our kids meeting in St. Louis for a weekend getaway. It thrilled my heart to see all four of our sons together having fun. I was the proud grandmother as I took my grandchildren to the kid's part of Six Flags St. Louis. We went on all kinds of rides together. It was wonderful spending three days with all of our kids.

When the kids left to head for home, Dave and I boarded a jumbo jet and headed to Las Vegas. We rented a car and began our journey to the Grand Canyon. I do not think I could have been more excited about anything in my life. I knew the presence of God would overwhelm me as I looked at His majesty.

We had one layover during our trip. Earlier thunderstorms cancelled some flights so our flight was delayed. As we sat together in the airport, a peaceful feeling overcame me as I realized I would have twelve days not to think about any of my years of learning, but to just have fun with my husband.

We finally arrived in Las Vegas and picked up a rental car. We put our luggage into the plush gray interior of our beautiful rental and we were off. Our long awaited vacation was beginning.

We were both tired yet excited. As I sat there in the passenger seat enjoying a warm bowl of soup, my heart was overwhelmed. The dark night with the shadows of the mountains had a certain mystery to them. The full moon was glistening over everything. It looked like the light of the moon was leading us to our destination. I felt so refreshed just resting my head on the headrest looking up into the sky.

A week of fun and rest was the reality we experienced. We saw the majesty of God everywhere. We visited the great Zion National Park and walked barefoot up a stream with a canyon of high mountains on either side of us. What an adventure.

The north and south sides of the Grand Canyon were more beautiful than words can describe. We experienced a sunrise and a sunset overlooking the canyon! Wow, can you imagine how awesome it was as the golden fireball slowly descended into the horizon? The presence of God was everywhere.

One morning I spent hours sitting on the edge of the mountains thinking about the past seventeen years and the journey I had been on. I had been in a learning room for fourteen of those years and the writing stage for three. The challenges of sitting still and listening to the still, small voice in my heart at times made me want to give up all that I felt I was supposed to do. I would cry out to God, "I cannot take anymore!" and He would lovingly send something or someone along to encourage me.

My journey took me to a foreign land, my dream city, a church, a business, and many other directions. At times I would obey the voice of God and other times I obeyed the voice of Robin, but God is faithful and He did not give up on me.

Was the learning worth it? I can honestly say I would not want to be the person I was before the long journey. I have learned how to have a beautiful relationship with the Creator of the universe. I have discovered that the Bible could SPEAK to me today, right where I am. I have realized that I will never hear the voice of God unless I STOP and communicate with Him.

I believe that God has a plan for everybody's future. You might have to go through a hard learning process, but when it arrives you will be grateful. When you begin to move out in the direction of the unknown, God will be there. You are never alone. He loves you more than you can imagine. He wants you to get to His plan as much as you want to get there, but we need to realize that we can throw obstacles in our own paths.

I have spent so many years wondering where God wanted me. I had dreams and plans of doing something great for God. My problem is that I spent so much time running around in circles, trying to figure it out. A line from another movie changed my life forever. The main character asked God, "How do you change the world?" God replied in a loving way, "With one Act of Random Kindness at a time."

These words ripped open my heart. I did not need to do GREAT things to change the world. All I need to do is to help each person that appears in my life, who might need encouragement, or a hug, or a listening ear, or a shoulder to cry on.

As I sat there on the edge of the Grand Canyon, a thought flashed across my mind. I was at THE END OF THE BEGINNING. I was at the END of ME, and my plans, and at the BEGINNING of total surrender to whatever plans God has for me.

HE IS SPEAKING!
I MUST TAKE THE TIME TO LISTEN.

QUESTION:

How can I have a relationship with God?

ANSWER:

All you need to do is ask Him.

If you desire to have a relationship with God, read the following verses from the Bible.

Romans 3:32

For ALL have sinned and fall short of the glory of God.

Everyone sins.

1 John 1:8-9

If we claim to be without sin, we deceive ourselves and the truth is not in us. If we confess our sins he is faithful and just and will forgive us our sins and cleanse us from all unrighteousness.

If we confess our sins, God will forgive us no matter what it is.

Romans 6:23

For the wages of sin is death, but the gift of God is eternal life through Jesus Christ our Lord.

We deserve to die for our sins, but God will give us eternal life through His son Jesus. If you would like to believe in God's gift of eternal life and begin a relationship with Him, read the following prayer.

Dear God,

I would like to begin a relationship with you. I know that I am a sinner, but the Bible tells me that you will forgive my sins, no matter what they are. Please forgive me of my sins and then help me to turn from them. I want you to be Lord of my life.

Maybe you began a relationship with God some time ago, but you have been neglecting building your relationship with Him. If you would like to start fresh in your relationship please read the following verse and prayer.

James 4:8a
Come near to God and He will come near to you.

Dear God,
I realize that a relationship with anyone requires speaking and listening to each other. Please forgive me for not taking the time to do this with you. Please help me to find my LISTENING Room and then make a commitment to SPEAK and LISTEN to you daily.

If you prayed either of these prayers I would love to hear about it. If you have any questions about this or anything in my book please Contact: Robinlee@hesspeakingarewelistening.com

<u>*Robin Gove's Family*</u>

Christmas 2006

Back Row, Left to right

Robin, Dave Sr., Jeremy, Andrew, Aaron & Katie, David & Stacy

Front Row: Brooke, Tyler, Streme

Robin & Dave
At the Grand Canyon

In Loving Memory of
Adeline Beck Nyberg
By Robin Gove

Her room was quiet as the sun peeked through the mini-blinds. I sat there all alone on the edge of the bed, holding her hand. She looked lifeless. The reality of "letting go" had set in, but how could I? She is my mother. I love her.

My thoughts went back to several months prior to this day when she could barely talk. She said to me, "Rob, when are you going to get busy and do something about your book?" (She was talking about this book.) She believed in me that I would one day finish it.

At that moment I felt compelled to lean down and whisper in her ear, "I will dedicate my writing to you, mom." I slowly put my lips to her face and gently kissed her. As I cupped my hands around her face, she opened her eyes and looked heavenward. Just like that she was ushered into Jesus' arms.

MOM, MY BOOK IS FINISHED!

Several months after she passed away, I wrote my first Bible Study called, "I have Lost Someone I Love." Since then I have written twenty He is <u>SPEAKING</u>! Are we <u>LISTENING</u>? Bible Studies that will be coming out in 2008, in loving memory of my mom.